HOW TO
SHARPEN
EVERY
BLADE
IN YOUR
WOODSHOP
DON GEARY

HOW TO
SHARPEN
EVERY
BLADE
IN YOUR
WOODSHOP

DON GEARY

BETTERWAY BOOKS
CINCINNATI, OHIO

Disclaimer

To prevent accidents, keep safety in mind while you work. Use the safety guards installed on power equipment; they are for your protection. When working on power equipment, keep fingers away from saw blades, wear safety goggles to prevent injuries from flying wood chips and sawdust, wear headphones to protect your hearing, and consider installing a dust vacuum to reduce the amount of airborne sawdust in your woodshop. Don't wear loose clothing, such as neckties or shirts with loose sleeves, or jewelry, such as rings, necklaces or bracelets, when working on power equipment, and tie back long hair to prevent it from getting caught in your equipment. The author and editors who compiled this book have tried to make all the contents as accurate and correct as possible. Plans, illustrations, photographs and text have been carefully checked. All instructions, plans and projects should be carefully read, studied and understood before beginning construction. Due to the variability of local conditions, construction materials, skills levels, etc., neither the authors nor Betterway books assumes any responsibility for any accidents, injuries, damages or other losses incurred resulting from the material presented in this book.

How to Sharpen Every Blade in Your Woodshop. Copyright © 1994 by Don Geary. Printed and bound in the United States of America. All rights reserved. No part of this book may be reproduced in any form or by any electronic or mechanical means including information storage and retrieval systems without permission in writing from the publisher, except by a reviewer, who may quote brief passages in a review. Published by Betterway Books, an imprint of F&W Publications, Inc., 1507 Dana Avenue, Cincinnati, Ohio 45207. (800) 289-0963. First edition.

Other fine Betterway Books are available from your local bookstore or direct from the publisher.

98 97   5 4 3

Library of Congress Cataloging-in-Publication Data

Geary, Don.
    How to sharpen every blade in your woodshop / by Don Geary.—1st ed.
        p.   cm.
    Includes index.
    ISBN 1-55870-342-X
    1. Woodworking tools—Amateurs' manuals. 2. Sharpening of tools—Amateurs' manuals. I. Title.
TT186.G43 1994
684'.08—dc20   94-18118
                                                       CIP

Betterway Books are available for sales promotions, premiums and fund-raising use. Special editions or book excerpts can also be created to specification. For details contact: Special Sales Manager, F&W Publications, 1507 Dana Avenue, Cincinnati, Ohio 45207.

Edited by R. Adam Blake
Interior design by Paul Neff

METRIC CONVERSION CHART		
TO CONVERT	**TO**	**MULTIPLY BY**
Inches	Centimeters	2.54
Centimeters	Inches	0.4
Feet	Centimeters	30.5
Centimeters	Feet	0.03
Yards	Meters	0.9
Meters	Yards	1.1
Sq. Inches	Sq. Centimeters	6.45
Sq. Centimeters	Sq. Inches	0.16
Sq. Feet	Sq. Meters	0.09
Sq. Meters	Sq. Feet	10.8
Sq. Yards	Sq. Meters	0.8
Sq. Meters	Sq. Yards	1.2
Pounds	Kilograms	0.45
Kilograms	Pounds	2.2
Ounces	Grams	28.4
Grams	Ounces	0.04

About the Author

Don Geary has been writing books and magazine articles for 20 years and specializes in home improvement, woodworking, tool working and related topics. He has been a member of the National Association of Home and Workshop Writers since 1976. Don also writes about the great outdoors and has been a member of the Outdoor Writer's Association since 1978.

Don lives with his wife and two sons in Salt Lake City, Utah where home and office are one in the same. Don's future writing plans call for more how-to books on home improvement and outdoor topics.

TABLE OF CONTENTS

INTRODUCTION

Woodworking has become a popular pastime, with more do-it-yourselfers getting involved every year. The variety of both hand and power tools available makes woodworking fun and can help you to achieve professional-looking results. New and better tools are introduced regularly and these greatly simplify many previously difficult tasks. One fact remains, however. For a tool to work most efficiently, it must be sharp. Learning the mechanics of sharpening is the main objective of this book.

We begin with a brief look at why it is important to keep tools sharp and in good condition. Then we look at the tools and machines that are used for grinding, sharpening, and restoring a cutting edge on all types of power and hand woodworking tools. The rest of the book covers how to sharpen specific tools that are common to woodworking shops—large and small. The book ends with suggestions for storing tools so they remain ready for use.

This book is designed to show you how to sharpen almost any woodworking tool that you may encounter, and it should be consulted before any sharpening task is attempted. Although there is nothing particularly difficult about sharpening in general, there is usually a special angle or sharpening technique that spells the difference between success and failure. I have tried to include such information wherever possible to aid you in sharpening common (and not-so-common) tools around the home workshop.

This information, coupled with a conscientious approach, will enable you to sharpen any given tool. After all is said and done, a sharp tool is a safe tool that will help you to accomplish a given task quickly and with predictable results.

It is my hope that you will learn in these pages not only how to sharpen a given tool but also come away with a clear understanding of just what a cutting edge is. Once you know the difference between a dull and sharp tool, you will never settle for anything but the keenest edge on any tool.

No book is solely the work of one person and this is certainly no exception. I extend thanks to the tool companies that have provided technical assistance, photographs and tools for photographic purposes. In alphabetical order these are: Black & Decker Corp.; Cooper Tools; DeWalt; Dremel; GATCO®; S-B Tool Company (formerly Skil Corp.); Sears, Roebuck and Co.; Stanley Tools; and Woodcraft Supply Corp.

I also thank my editor, Adam Blake, for encouragement during this project, and Mary Lang for help with a number of the illustrations in the book. Last, I thank my wife, Susan, for loving support and understanding. She well knows that it is not easy to be married to a freelance writer.

Don Geary
Salt Lake City, Utah, 1994

CHAPTER ONE
Get the Edge

Almost any tool has a cutting or working edge; for the tool to work efficiently, this edge must be maintained. A dull saw blade, for example, will burn, rip, and require much more effort to use. A sharp saw blade, on the other hand, will slice cleanly through a piece of lumber with little effort on the part of the user or the power tool.

A tool can be depended on to become dull with use; this is normal and should be expected. Usually your first clue is more effort required on your part to accomplish a given task. Other indicators include rough edges on a cut—as with a saw or chisel—or in extreme cases, tearing rather than cutting and burning around the cut area.

A tool's dullness (as with a twist drill bit) may not be so obvious when used in a power tool. A power tool does the muscle work and therefore has a tendency to overcome dullness through sheer force. Once a tool becomes dull, however, the need to sharpen it will become known rather quickly as more effort on your part will be required to do the work or the work does not turn out the way you expected.

Never assume that because a tool is new it will be sharp. I have used brand new saw blades right out of the package that did not cut as well as the one that was just replaced. Upon examination, I found that one new blade—either because of poor workmanship or inspection—had teeth that had missed the sharpening step at the factory, and in another case, teeth that were all set to one side. When set properly, teeth alternate, left and right.

This does not mean that all new tools are dull when purchased, but look them over carefully before use. As a rule, you can expect that a quality tool for which you paid handsomely should perform as expected right out of the box. After all, that is why we spend dearly for high-quality tools. Also, modern manufacturing processes and quality checks—from reputable manufacturers—almost ensure that a given tool will work perfectly from the start. Nevertheless, check new tools before use and touch up as needed.

Sharp tools are much more enjoyable to use than dull ones. A sharp saw blade will slice cleanly through wood with little effort on your part or from the saw motor. A sharp chisel will help you to make a square mortise hole, while a dull chisel will make the work look like you used a hatchet instead. A sharp drill bit will bore a clean, precise hole, whereas a dull bit will make a hole that looks more like the work was shot with a bullet rather than bored.

In addition to helping you to do better work, sharp tools are much safer to use than dull ones. Although it is true that a dull tool will cut you just as easily as a sharp one, the chances of mishap are greater with dull tools, because they require more effort to use. When a tool is forced, it is more prone to slip.

Lastly, sharp tools save time and money as well

as effort. A sharp tool will do a job right the first time, cutting for example, but a dull tool often produces unacceptable results. A dull tool will cause wasted materials, extra effort and frustration.

Anatomy of a Cutting Edge

If you were to look at a sharp cutting edge under a microscope, you would see an edge that more resembled a Stone Age tool rather than what you expected. Instead of a keen edge, you would see a raggedy line of peaks and troughs. If you were to look at a dull cutting edge under the same microscopic power, you would see a really rough edge composed of very deep troughs and irregular peaks. The major difference, of course, is that the sharp edge has the ability to cut or shave while the dull edge is only capable of tearing the work.

Although it is true that a sharp edge will dull with use, a dull edge can only become worse. Sharpening reduces the overall roughness of a cutting edge and enables the tool to cut rather than tear. Even though a sharpened edge appears rough under a microscope, it is less rough than the material being worked and therefore has the ability to cut or peel away the surface smoothly.

When a dull tool is sharpened, the main idea is to reduce the difference between the high and low spots on the cutting edge. When sharpening is undertaken often, this can usually be accomplished by whetting only the edge bevel of the tool. The correct edge bevel of a tool is important. If the tool has sustained damage—a nick, for example—the edge must be ground to a point just below the damage. As a rule, the less metal removed in the sharpening process the longer the tool will last.

You must remember that the roughness of a sharp blade is microscopically small. If roughness is present that you can see with the naked eye, the blade is damaged and must be reground before you

attempt sharpening. A nicked or chipped blade must be ground back far enough to remove the damage. In some cases this may involve reshaping the edge bevel, but this is not difficult on modern grinders equipped with an abrasive grinding wheel.

Cleaning

In many cases a tool may not be as dull as it is dirty. A gummed-up saw blade, for example, may bind up in the work or require more effort to use. Often a thorough cleaning will help to restore the tool to proper working condition quickly. A careful inspection of a tool that seems dull may often reveal that it is dirty or, in extreme cases, rusty.

Router bits, saw blades (both electric and hand-held), planer blades and other cutter tools will all accumulate pitch and become encrusted with sawdust over time. To work most effectively, this residue must be removed or heat will build up on the tool and it will not work well and will, in fact, dull quickly.

Special cleaning liquids are available for removing pitch residue and hardened sawdust from cutting tools. Lacking one of these cleaners, you can substitute turpentine. Allow the tool—router bit, drill bit, saw blade, for example—to soak for several hours in the liquid and then scrub with a stiff bristle brush. Clean with soapy water, dry, and apply a light spray of silicone to protect against rust. This treatment will not only clean a pitch-coated tool but will also make it run cooler and cut more efficiently.

Storage

Remember that tools can easily be dulled during storage or transit and should therefore be protected from damage. This is most easily accomplished by storing cutting tools in protective cases when not in use. Special carrying cases and storage cabinets (or at least a drawer) will also do much to ensure that your cutting and boring tools are sharp and ready for use. See chapter twelve for details on storage.

CHAPTER TWO
Tools for Sharpening

There is a vast selection of tools and accessories designed to help with sharpening around the home and workshop. Although it is possible to accomplish a wide range of sharpening tasks with a simple pocket stone, you will find sharpening in general easier and more efficient if you choose the right sharpening tool for the task at hand. This can be somewhat confusing when you consider that there are probably hundreds of different sharpening tools available.

The list of sharpening tools includes a wide variety of sharpening stones (both man-made and natural), files, abrasive papers, hones, slip stones, stops, files, sharpening steels and grinding wheels. Add to this a bewildering array of sharpening aids, guides, electronic devices and other gizmos, and it is easy to understand why the average person has no idea of just what the "right" sharpening tool for a particular task may be. In this chapter we look at sharpening tools and explain the use of each. In the end you should have a clear understanding of which sharpening tool to choose for any given sharpening task.

Sharpening Stones

Many types, shapes and sizes of sharpening stones are available, and undoubtedly there are several good choices for almost any sharpening project. In general, all sharpening stones fall into one of two rather large groups: natural and man-made.

Natural sharpening stones are, as the name suggests, stones that are found in nature. Some of the more familiar ones include emery (which has probably been used for the longest period of time), garnet, quartz and several blue stone abrasives, which are found in the states of Arkansas and Ohio. Later in this chapter we will discuss the more popular of these natural stones in detail.

Man-made sharpening stones are generally harder than natural sharpening stones (except, of course, for diamond-dust abrasives, which are the hardest of all abrasives). In addition, man-made sharpening stones are uniform in grit size. This small fact may not seem very important at first, but having uniform grit throughout a sharpening stone makes predictable sharpening possible. Natural sharpening stones do not have this degree of uniformity. For this reason, man-made stones are preferable for most sharpening tasks. In addition, man-made sharpening stones are commonly less expensive than natural stones.

All man-made sharpening stones are composed of two basic parts: the *abrasive*, and a *bonding agent*, which holds the grains of abrasive in a usable form (such as a sharpening stone or grinding wheel). Each of these parts is equally important.

Abrasives

The abrasive grains in a sharpening stone (and in grinding wheels as well) are the elements that actually perform the cutting during the sharpening process. During the sharpening operation, these grains fracture, resulting in a new cutting surface or edge. This means that there is an almost continual rejuvenation of the sharpening stone's surface, ensuring that the stone is accomplishing the sharpening task as best as possible. Eventually, individual grains of abrasive fracture to the point where they can no longer cut. When this happens, the adhesive releases its hold and the useless grain of abrasive is allowed to float free on the surface where it is carried away by the oil used during the sharpening. This is an ongoing process, and abrasive particles from below take over the cutting or sharpening as needed. Since all man-made sharpening stones are composed of millions of abrasive particles, you can reasonably expect such a stone to perform well for a very long period of time.

It is now possible to manufacture man-made sharpening stones in an almost infinite variety of abrasive grain sizes and types. The larger the abrasive grain size, the faster it will cut or remove metal from a tool's cutting edge, but this will also result in a rough texture on the metal being sharpened. Fine abrasive grit sizes, on the other hand, remove less material and result in a metal surface that is much smoother, to the point of polishing rather than actually removing much metal from the tool being sharpened.

The making of man-made sharpening stones is an interesting process. First raw materials, such as silicon carbide and aluminum oxide, are crushed in a milling machine to break up the pieces into a variety of grit sizes.

After the raw material has been crushed, it is passed through a series of screens to sort it by grit size. The ultimate grit size is determined by the number of meshes per linear inch in the screen used

A variety of sharpening aids, such as this circular saw blade jointer, is currently available for the do-it-yourself sharpener.

to separate the various grains. Finer grit sizes are separated by hydraulic or air classification methods. Sizes of grit range from 4 to 1,000 with the coarse grains having the lower number.

Various abrasive grain-like materials are used to make sharpening stones and grinding wheels. Let's look at these to see what is currently available for sharpening.

Aluminum Oxide

Aluminum oxide is a manufactured abrasive produced by fusing bauxite in an electric furnace at a temperature of about 3,700°F. During a typical run, fresh supplies of bauxite are added to the furnace

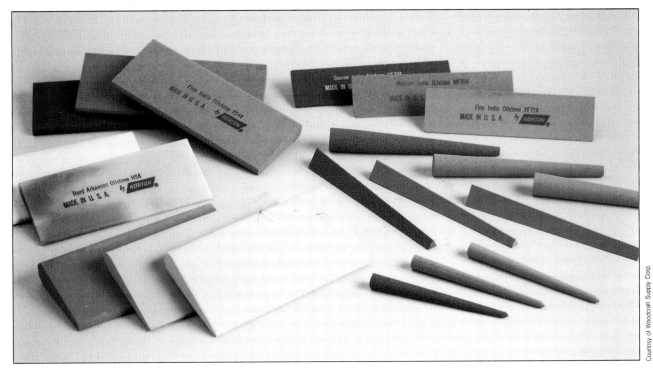

continually. The finished product is a large "pig" of crystalline aluminum oxide, which is then broken up, crushed, and sized to various usable grain sizes. This sizing is done by passing the pulverized aluminum oxide abrasive grains through various sizes of mesh screening that effectively separates the grains by size. Aluminum oxide abrasive is a tough, sharp grain bearing the chemical formula Al_2O_3.

Silicon Carbide

Silicon carbide abrasive is made by converting pure silica sand and petroleum coke into silicon carbide in a resistant-type electric furnace at approximately 4,000°F. After cooling, the resulting mass is broken up, carefully sorted, crushed and sized to a usable range of grit sizes. Silicon carbide is harder and sharper than aluminum oxide. The chemical formula for silicon carbide is SiC.

Diamond

Diamonds are the hardest material known to man and are almost pure carbon crystal. Both natural

A vast selection of sharpening stones — both natural and man-made — is easily available.

diamonds and manufactured (synthetic) diamonds are used for making sharpening stones and grinding wheels. Natural diamonds are used in both resin- and metal-bonded diamond grinding wheels. Man-made or manufactured diamonds in suitable sizes and shapes are the choice for resin-bonded diamond grinding wheels and sharpening stones. These types of diamonds are best for sharpening or grinding all carbide materials.

Cubic Boron Nitride

Cubic-structured boron nitride is a man-made abrasive that approaches the diamond in hardness. It was developed as an outgrowth of synthetic diamond research by the General Electric Company (GE) and is marketed in the United States by GE Superabrasives under the trade name Borazon™ CBN.

Abrasive Adhesives

The second part of any man-made sharpening stone or grinding wheel (in addition to the abrasive itself) is the adhesive or bonding agent used to hold the grains together in a usable form. At present, five major bonding agents are used in the industry and we will briefly discuss each of these.

Resinoid

Resinoid is a thermosetting resin. Resin-bonded grinding wheels are extremely durable and can be operated at high speeds — up to 16,000 square feet per minute (sfpm). Since this bonding agent is capable of withstanding severe and abusive grinding stresses, resinoid grinding wheels are currently the choice for high-speed rough grinding and cutoff operations. They are also made with fine grits to produce super finishes on some precision grinding jobs. For certain applications, resinoid grinding wheels are reinforced for added strength.

Vitrified

Glassy-type, clay-type and porcelaneous-type bonds are used in the manufacture of vitrified bonding grinding wheels and sharpening stones. More than half of all grinding wheels made today are of the many types of vitrified bonds. Their rigidity provides fast, economical stock removal and makes them especially well suited to precision grinding up to about 12,000 sfpm as well as other general-purpose grinding operations. Most sharpening stones are made using this bonding method.

Rubber

Both natural and synthetic rubbers are used as bonds in the manufacture of grinding wheels and sharpening stones. In softer types, the resiliency of this bond produces excellent polishing wheels. The harder types combine a degree of resiliency and water resistance for safe, cool-cutting cutoff wheels which are used when burr and burn of the metal must be held to a minimum.

Shellac

Shellac makes a low-heat-resistant bond resulting in very versatile grinding action, with particular qualities of free-cutting action and good finish. Shellac generally has very limited use, mainly in the manufacture of roll grinding wheels. Roll grinding wheels are cylindrical in shape and are used for special-purpose grinding and sharpening.

Metal

Metal is used as a bonding agent only in the manufacture of diamond grinding wheels and sharpening stones. When metal bonding is used it is strong, ductile, and as you might expect, costly.

Sharpening stones, both man-made and natural, come in a variety of shapes, sizes and configurations. The most basic of all are the common bench stones that are simply rectangular. In addition, there are rounded, curved, tapered and even grooved sharpening stone designs. As a rule, the stone's intended purpose will usually dictate the design and composition. For example, to put an edge on a knife, a flat bench stone is the best choice, but for sharpening a scythe (which has a curved blade and only one sharpened side) a special oval-shaped stone is a far better choice. Throughout this book, when I talk about performing a sharpening operation with a stone, I will point out the recommended stone shape, size and type for that particular sharpening task.

Grinding Wheels

Modern grinding wheels can remove large amounts of metal quickly and are therefore useful during some sharpening operations, especially when a tool edge has been chipped or otherwise damaged. As a rule, however, grinding wheels work too quickly for standard sharpening tasks, such as putting a keen edge on a knife. This task is better accomplished on a common bench stone. In addition, if a grinding wheel is used incorrectly, you run the risk of overheating the tool and ruining its *temper* — the existing hardness of the metal. As a rule, if a piece of tool steel is heated up to a straw color — an easy task on a modern grinding wheel — the temper of the tool's steel will have been changed and, as a result, it will never be

the same again. It is therefore possible to ruin a tool by trying to sharpen it on a grinding wheel.

Grinding wheels do play an important part in reshaping tool edges prior to sharpening with a slower-working sharpening stone, providing that the proper grinding wheel is used for the work. At the present, almost all grinding wheels are man-made and there are hundreds of different types to choose from. For this reason we need talk a bit about how grinding wheels are made, graded and properly used.

The production and manufacture of modern grinding wheels are the result of many years of research and experience. All grinding wheels can rightly be considered precision cutting tools and are made according to specific industry-wide standards. As a result, grinding wheels are uniform throughout and

A good selection of bench stones helps you tackle any sharpening task.

can be relied upon to perform well throughout their range of capabilities.

The process of manufacturing modern grinding wheels begins by measuring precise amounts of abrasive grains of a uniform size. As mentioned earlier, grains of abrasive material are separated by passing the material through different sizes of mesh screening. Electronically controlled automatic weighing and mixing operations ensure that each grinding wheel is made up of exactly the right ingredients; uniformity

Always work carefully on a bench grinder to avoid damaging the temper of a tool by excessive heat.

throughout each wheel is guaranteed. Next, the abrasive grit is mixed with a bonding material—resinoid, vitrified, rubber, shellac or metal, as described earlier in this chapter. These two ingredients are mixed thoroughly and screened once again until complete uniformity is achieved. Then the abrasive-bonding-agent mixture is pressed into a special mold that is

Courtesy of Woodcraft Supply Corp.

Grinding wheels come in a wide range of grit sizes and composition.

in the shape of the desired grinding wheel. Within the molds, the mixture is hydraulically pressed to exact density or grain spacing. This grain spacing is commonly referred to as the "structure" of the grinding wheel and it is a very important step in the manufacturing process, which we will cover later in this section.

The welding of the abrasive grit and bonding agent is achieved with heat in either kilns (which achieve high temperatures) or ovens (which offer much lower temperatures). Vitrified bonded grinding wheels are processed at temperatures approaching 2,300°F (in kilns), while other bonding agents (such as resin, rubber or shellac) are heated in ovens that do not reach temperatures much above 400°F.

Hardness and grade of every grinding wheel is monitored throughout the manufacturing process by various means, including stroboscopic (spin testing) and sonic (sound penetration) testing equipment and, in some cases, sophisticated machine penetration. If bushings, steel backs or other mounting devices are required, these are secured after the grinding wheel has been fired. The next steps in the process include spin testing of all grinding wheels, further grading

and labeling.

Grinding wheels are labeled according to a marking system that is standard throughout the industry. It is possible, for example, to look at any grinding wheel made in the United States and determine its makeup, grade, bonding agent type, etc. The chart below shows the order of grinding wheel markings currently in use.

Earlier I mentioned grain structure in grinding wheels; let's examine a few points about this. In analyzing grinding wheel grain structure, it is important to understand that abrasive grain size (for a given grinding wheel) remains constant. However, the volume of the abrasive grain will vary according to the structure of that particular wheel. For example, the volume of abrasive grain is greater in a dense-structured wheel and the volume is less in open-structured grinding wheels.

As a rule, closer grain spacing is denoted by low structure numbers and such a wheel is regarded as being dense. Higher structure numbers indicate a more open grain spacing, or less density. It is important to keep in mind that the amount of space around each grain of abrasive grit is predetermined and achieved by the bonding agent and the amount of hydraulic pressure applied to the abrasive-bonding-agent mixture when it is poured into the mold. These spaces, or voids, around the abrasive grains allow the grains to escape as they become dull and useless in cutting or sharpening. The sharpness of the individual abrasive grains, the bonding agent used, and the

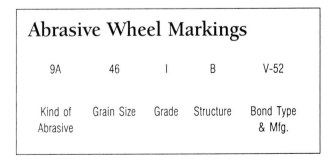

Abrasive Wheel Markings				
9A	46	I	B	V-52
Kind of Abrasive	Grain Size	Grade	Structure	Bond Type & Mfg.

Standard markings for abrasive wheels used in grinders.

Silicone carbide composition grinding wheels are available in three grades — fine, medium and coarse — and are durable as well as relatively inexpensive.

intended application of the grinding wheel all are important factors in determining how the wheel is put together.

As with sharpening stones, grinding wheels are made from abrasive grains from four basic materials: aluminum oxide, silicon carbide, diamonds and cubic boron nitride. Since there are differences in physical properties between grinding wheel materials, it will be helpful to briefly mention how each type is used.

Aluminum oxide grinding wheels probably account for the largest part of grinding wheel makeup. In fact, if one wheel could be considered general purpose, aluminum oxide would be the choice. Generally speaking, aluminum oxide grinding wheels are used for grinding all steel alloys.

Silicon carbide grinding wheels are the second most popular type; because of their strength and quick cutting ability, they are used for grinding a wide range of hard and dense materials. The list includes all nonferrous metals (aluminum, brass, copper and bronze), cast and chilled iron, and most types of nonmetallic materials such as glass, stone and ceramics.

Diamond grinding wheels are very hard and are used extensively in industry. They are ideal for grinding very hard materials such as carbide, cemented carbide, stainless steel and high-carbon steel. Because diamond grinding wheels are expensive, it is probably a safe assumption that the average do-it-yourselfer will not have one to work with.

Cubic boron nitride, as mentioned earlier, is a man-made abrasive material that approaches the diamond in hardness. Since this material is not as expensive as diamond abrasive, it is used with greater frequency both in industry and at the consumer level.

Cubic boron nitride grinding wheels are a good choice for grinding and sharpening very hard ferrous metals such as carbide, stainless steel and high-carbon steel.

Although hundreds of different grinding wheel shapes, sizes and designs are available, the home sharpener needs to know about only a few basic types. These include the straight, straight cup and possibly flared cup designs. In fact, almost all home grinding can be done with a straight grinding wheel design. This is a good choice, as the straight design is readily available in a wide range of abrasives and grit sizes.

Bench Grinders

To take full advantage of modern grinding wheels, the do-it-yourselfer should have a good bench grinding machine. This electric tool can be used for a number of grinding tasks around the home workshop and it is therefore important that you exercise a certain amount of care when buying one. At present, there are a number of good bench grinders available.

Modern bench grinders are rated according to how large a grinding wheel can be used on the machine. At present, these sizes range from the small 5″ unit to the 8″ heavy-duty models. In addition, all electric grinders also have a horsepower rating—about ¼ hp for the small hobbyist versions up to 1 hp for larger, heavy-duty bench grinders.

Probably the best all-around bench grinder for the do-it-yourselfer is one with a horsepower rating of from ½ to ¾ hp. Such a grinder will take grinding wheels up to 6″ × ¾″ and be powerful enough for all grinding tasks around the home. In addition, there are a few other features that you will find useful on a bench grinder. These include a special gooseneck light on the machine, so you can see clearly as you work; adjustable tool rests in front of each wheel, which enable you to perform precision grinding; ad-justable and adequate clear plastic eye shields; and easily removable wheel covers (shielding for the sides of the grinding wheels). A bench grinder with these features and attachments should cost about a hundred dollars—a small price for a machine that should last many years under normal home workshop working conditions.

Before using it, you must securely fasten your grinder to a workbench or special stand. This will not only enable you to use the grinder safely, but it also helps you to take full advantage of its capabilities. When mounting your grinder to a workbench, position it close to the edge and far enough away from the walls so that you can lift long tools up for grinding, if needed. Although a bench grinder is handy for many projects around the home, you probably will not use it as frequently as other tools around the shop. For this reason, it is always best to locate your grinder so that it will not be in the way when you work on other projects in the home workshop. The end of a workbench is the usual and most common location of a bench grinder.

One very good alternative to mounting your grinder on the workbench is to make or buy a special stand for it. Several good steel grinder stands are available from national tool chain stores (such as Sears Roebuck) and through mail order. Some versions of grinder stands are mounted on wheels so the unit can be moved around the shop as needed.

Bench Grinder Safety

Grinding metal is a task that should never be approached casually, as the potential for injury always exists. Before attaching a new (or previously used) abrasive wheel to the grinder, there are a few things that you should do. In addition, always take safety precautions whenever attempting any grinding task.

Abrasive wheels for bench grinding machines can be damaged easily if dropped, so it is important to handle them carefully. Before you mount a grinding

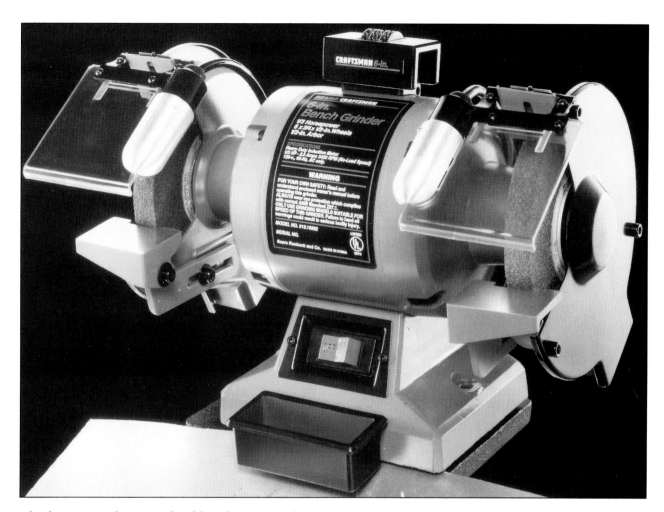

wheel on a grinder, you should make certain that the wheel is in sound condition. This can easily be accomplished by tapping the wheel with a light wooden or plastic tool. The handle of a screwdriver works well for this. Suspend the wheel by slipping the blade of a screwdriver through the center hole and then gently tap the side of the wheel in four places — north, south, east and west, for example. Each tap should produce a clear ring. If the tapping does not produce a ringing sound, look the stone over *very* carefully to check for small cracks or fissures.

When performing the ring test on a grinding wheel, it is important to know that different abrasive materials will produce rings with different tones. To give you some basis for comparison, know that vitrified and silicate wheels emit a clear metallic ring. Organic-bonded wheels, on the other hand, usually give a less clear ring, but it will be a ring nevertheless.

A good grinder will have an adjustable tool rest, side covers and eye shields.

A dull, nonmetallic ring usually means that the wheel has a crack. In addition, oil- or water-soaked wheels do not ring clearly. Grinding wheels that have been soaked or filled by the manufacturer to modify the cutting action of the wheel will sound dull, but there will still be a ringing sound. Obviously, if a dead sound is produced by the tap test, you should inspect the grinding wheel for cracks. *If any cracks are found, do not use the wheel on a grinding machine.* The chances are good of it flying apart when subjected to the high rpm's of standard bench grinders. If the wheel has never been used, return it to the manufacturer for a replacement. If the grinding wheel is used or old, discard it. Of course, you can use a damaged grinding wheel as a bench stone, but never on a grinding machine.

When mounting a sound grinding wheel on a grinding machine, there are a few things you must do to ensure that the task is done correctly. Since all straight abrasive wheels are mounted between two flanges, the actual fastening is fairly straightforward. It is important that both flanges be of the same diameter and perfectly true. In addition, the flanges should not be less than one-third the diameter of the abrasive wheel being attached.

Tighten flange nuts only enough to hold the wheel firmly in position and to prevent slippage. Do not overtighten; this may distort the flanges or, worse yet, crack the abrasive wheel.

After mounting an abrasive wheel on the grinding machine, reattach the wheel guards. When grinding wheels are not shielded properly with side covers, personal injury is possible due to flying bits of ground metal or, in extreme cases, when a grinding wheel blows apart.

Before you begin working on a grinding wheel, make sure you have plenty of work space around the machine. This will generally mean clearing the area around the machine. In addition, provide good lighting—both general shop lighting and specific lighting around the grinder.

When actually working on a bench grinder, always wear suitable eye protection. This may be a pair of plastic lens goggles or a face shield. It is a good safety practice to keep some type of eye protection on top of the grinding machine. This way you will be reminded to protect your eyes before turning the machine on. Do not rely solely on the plastic shields that are on most modern grinders. Although these clear plastic shields offer some protection against flying metal particles, they are inadequate as far as proper eye protection is concerned.

As you grind, work only on the front edge of the abrasive wheel. It is generally agreed that no grinding should be done on the side of the wheel, as this will put undue strain on the wheel and in-

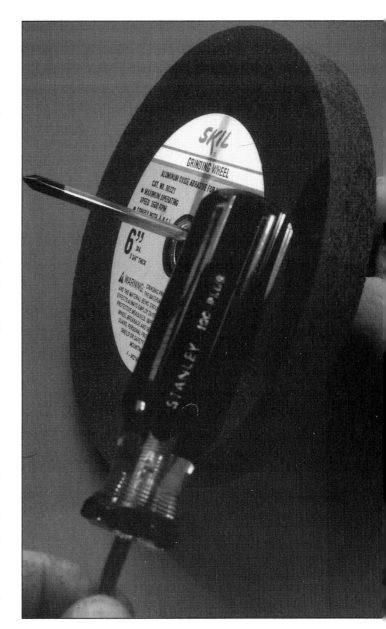

Tap a grinding wheel with the handle of a screwdriver before installing on a grinder. A clear "ring" indicates that the wheel is in sound condition.

crease the chances that it will break. Also, when grinding, it is important not to force work into the spinning wheel; this will put excess strain on the wheel as well.

Check the condition of your abrasive wheel often, especially when you are doing a lot of grinding. Occasionally the face of the wheel will clog with metal. When this happens, the face of the wheel will

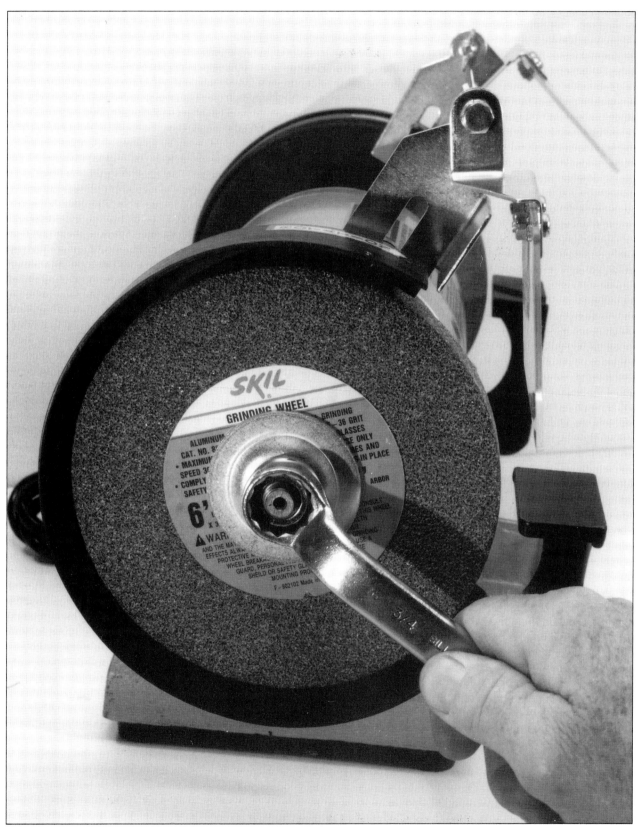

A new grinding wheel is bolted on the grinder drive shaft.

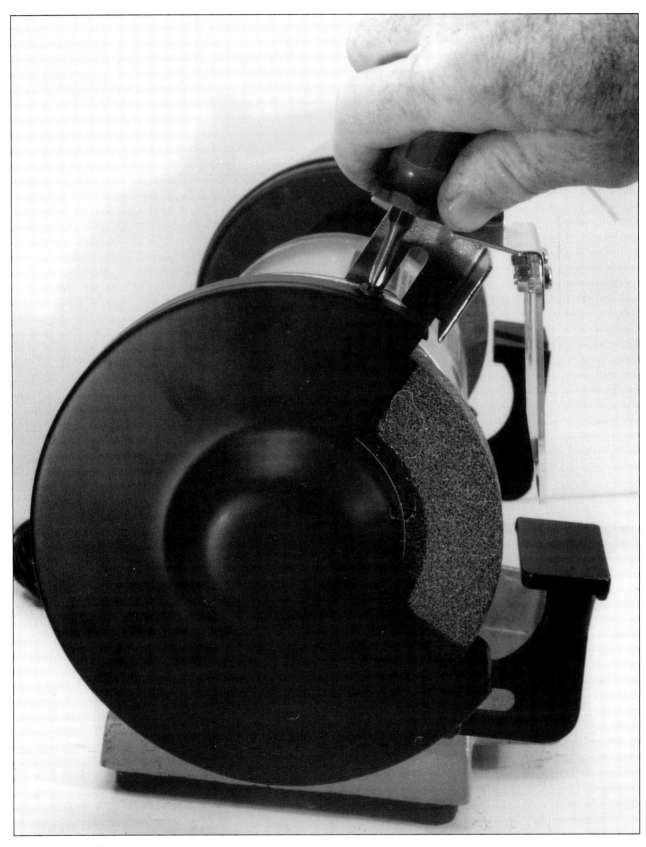

For safety's sake, never operate a bench grinder
without side covers in place.

appear glazed and you will also notice that more pressure is required to grind. The best way to clean up a clogged abrasive grinding wheel is to use a special wheel dresser. This is simply a carbide wheel mounted on the end of a tool that is pressed into the spinning wheel and that effectively rejuvenates it. With a minimum of care, a quality grinding wheel should provide years of service in the home workshop.

Files

Another type of tool that is useful for some sharpening tasks is the file. A file can remove large amounts of metal from a tool edge quickly. Unlike a grinding wheel, however, a file will not generally heat up metal during the process. For this reason, a file is often a good choice for restoring or reshaping tasks. In some cases, a file is the tool used for the sharpening task— sharpening a chainsaw, for example. At other times, a file is used for developing an edge on a tool prior to final sharpening with a stone. An ax or adze are good examples of this.

To the untrained eye, all files are the same, but to the experienced, there are a number of differences between them. Basically, files are grouped into two general categories—single-cut and double-cut files. For our purposes, this simply indicates the direction of lines on the face of a file. On a single-cut file, all the lines run in one direction across the face of the file. On double-cut files, these lines cross or are intersected by other lines with the overall effect of an "×" or basket-weave pattern.

All files are made from very hard tool steel, a fact that makes the removal of metal with this tool possible. As you might have guessed, several different types of steel alloys are used in file production, but we will not get very far into metallurgy in these pages.

The do-it-yourself home sharpener should be familiar with several file shapes or designs. These in-

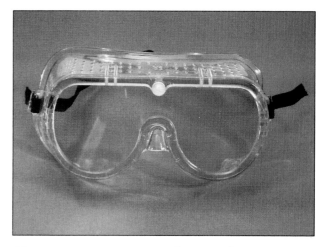

Always use eye protection when grinding.

clude the flat, round, triangular and tapered files. All these basic file shapes are readily available wherever files are sold. Each of these files is designed for general use, as well as for specific applications. For example, a round file can be used to sharpen the teeth in a saw chain, but can also be used to file the gullets on a handsaw or circular saw blade. A triangular file is commonly used to sharpen or touch up the edges of a handsaw's teeth, but can also be used on circular saw blade teeth. It is therefore important to choose the right file for the sharpening task at hand, provided that the task does indeed require a specially shaped or designed file. The chart on page 19 lists the proper files for saw sharpening.

In addition to choosing the right basic type of file for the task at hand, it is equally important to use the file properly. Most people who are not familiar with file use approach the task incorrectly. It is a fact that a file works best when pushed slowly into the work, and this is the best way to work a file— with slow, firm, deliberate strokes.

A file should never be used without a handle. Ironically, files are almost never sold with a handle. Instead, we find a selection of files and a selection of file handles. I suppose the reasoning behind this is that the file will wear out before the handle, so one handle can be used for a long line of files. In any event, never attempt to use a file without a

Courtesy of Woodcraft Supply Corp.

A diamond point wheel dresser will recondition a worn or clogged grinding wheel.

handle. Either purchase a few wooden or plastic file handles (they should last a lifetime) or make wooden handles in the workshop. Personally I prefer commercially made wooden handles. They are inexpensive and do the job of holding a file quite nicely, but you might want to make a few handles in the shop.

The simplest of all file handles are made from wooden dowels. For small files, ¾" diameter dowels are ideal; larger dowels—up to about 1½" in diameter—are great for big files. Large wooden dowels also make great handles for large woodworking rasps—those gnarly toothed, file-like tools that are used for various shaping tasks in woodworking. The length of each handle should be approximately 4" for the average size hand. If your hands are smaller or larger,

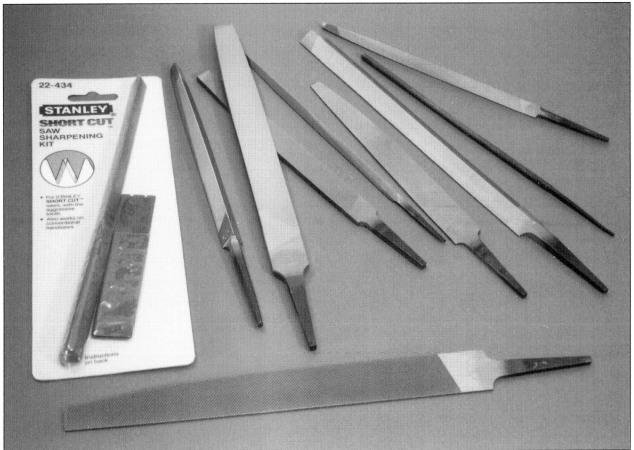

A variety of files can be used for sharpening.

Files for Saw Sharpening

Handsaws:

Crosscut 5 point and 5½ point	6″ regular taper file
Crosscut 6, 7, 8 and 9 point	4½″ regular taper file
Crosscut 10, 11 and 12 point	5½″ slim taper file
Rip 4½, 5, 5½ and 6 point	4½″ regular taper file
Coarse rip 4 point	6″ regular taper file

Circular Saw Blades:

Gullets	6″ round chain saw file
Jointing	6″ or 8″ flat file
Teeth	6″ or 8″ flat mill file

Choose the right file for saw tooth sharpening.
Points are tooth points per inch.
Files: Regular taper is a file that is tapered toward the tip; slim taper is a thin version; flat file is flat on top and bottom and can be rounded or square on edges; mill file has teeth that have been milled into the surface rather than cut; chain saw file is used for sharpening a saw chain. These are standard call names for files that are readily available.

adjust the length of your file handles to fit your hand comfortably.

After cutting a dowel to the desired length, drill a suitable hole in one end to accommodate the tang (pointed) end of a file. For small files, a hole about ⅛″ inch in diameter is suitable, but for larger files you will probably need a hole at least ¼″ in diameter. After a hole has been drilled in one end, round off the other end with a wood rasp. Finish off the job with fine sandpaper and you can consider the handle ready for service.

Two added touches that will increase the life of your homemade file handles are to paint them and wrap wire around the hole end. The wire will help to prevent the handle from cracking in the event that the file is pushed too firmly into the handle. Bright

acrylic paints look good on file handles and will also make them easier to clean with a cloth.

A file will rust if it becomes wet and is then exposed to the atmosphere. One method used by some to prevent this is to spray files with a silicone spray such as WD-40. Such a lubricant will not affect how the file works but will effectively prevent rust.

As a file is used to remove metal from a tool edge, the grooves in the face of the file often become clogged with tiny bits of metal. When this happens, the file is much less effective at cutting. If the file is not cleaned at this point it will not cut and will be useless. The only solution to this clogging problem is to clean the grooves in the file face. Although there are several ways of doing this, the best involves the use of a special brush called a *file card*. This file-cleaning tool is a good investment for the home craftsman because it will effectively extend the life of any file by keeping the grooves clean and sharp.

To use a file card, brush the grooves on the file face with the steel bristles on one side of the card. The steel bristles scrub out the grooves and make them almost as good as new. As you brush the grooves, you will see tiny bits of metal coming free. After cleaning the file in this manner, turn the file card over — the other side contains stiff fiber bristles — and brush the file again. The fiber bristles remove all of those tiny metal bits that the eye cannot detect. Generally speaking, a file will be almost as good as new after it has been cleaned with a file card.

Lubricants

Whenever a bench sharpening stone is used for putting an edge on a tool, some type of lubricant should also be used. A variety of lubricants can be used during sharpening, and almost anyone who is familiar with sharpening on a stone has a favorite to use.

Probably the best stone lubricant to use for sharpening is one of the many oils offered by sharpening

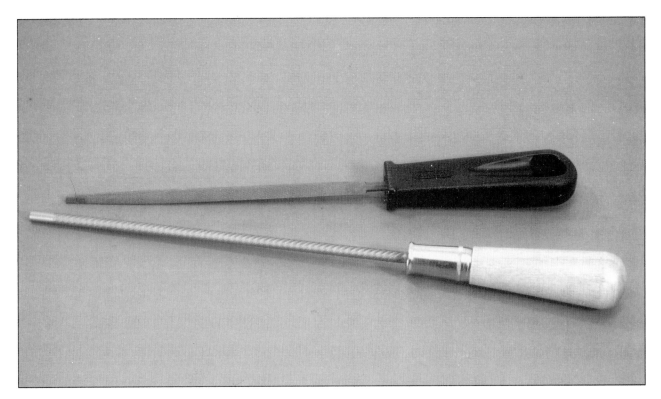

stone manufacturers. These are generally referred to as *honing oils*. When such an oil is not available, you can use almost any lightweight oil as a substitute. The choices include cooking oil, olive oil, medicinal mineral oil, sewing machine oil and even kerosene. If nothing else is available, use clear water to help lubricate the stone.

Lubricants play a very important part in the sharpening process (when using a sharpening stone), so it is necessary to use some type of oil. Oil on the surface of a sharpening stone helps to float off metal and abrasive dust that would otherwise become imbedded in the surface of the stone. If this were to happen, the stone would become clogged on the surface and useless at sharpening. One hard-and-fast rule about sharpening on a bench stone, then, is *always use some type of lubricating oil on the stone.*

A new sharpening stone should also be soaked in oil before use (unless, of course, the stone has been oil-filled by the manufacturer). Soaking a bench stone in oil makes it easier to use and thus a more effective sharpening tool. Probably the best way to soak a stone is to place it in a small container and

File handles — made from plastic or wood — make file use much easier.

let it soak overnight in a lightweight mineral oil. After this initial soaking, wipe off the excess oil before use. During use, apply a few drops of oil to the surface of the stone as usual to help carry off abrasive dust and tiny bits of metal on the surface.

After using a bench stone for sharpening, wipe it off with a clean rag. Before you put it away, apply a few drops of clean oil to the surface. Store in a covered wooden box or in a plastic bag. Covered storage is important, as dust and airborne material will clog the surface of a stone just as surely as abrasive dust and metal.

With time, all stones develop a slight indented curve. This is a result of the nature of the work that sharpening stones are called upon to do, and is quite normal. Nevertheless, a "bellied" stone is difficult to sharpen on, so you should make the surface flat by sanding before using the stone for a sharpening task. In some extreme cases it is best to simply purchase a new combination stone rather than try to flatten a

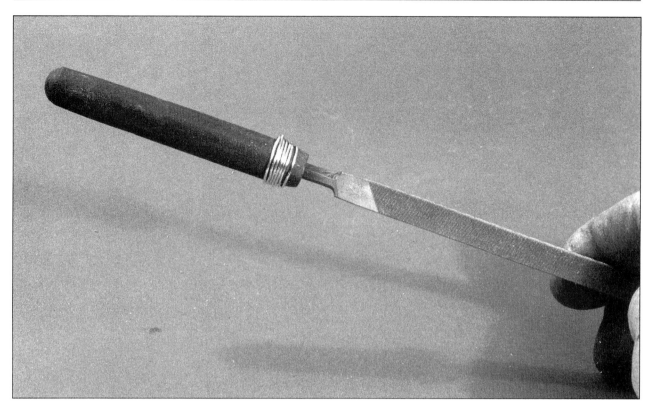

Make custom file handles from wooden dowels.

A file card is very useful for cleaning up a clogged file.

well-used stone.

To check the flatness of the surface of a bench stone—and *always* suspect old stones as being bellied—lay it on a flat piece of 80 grit sandpaper and rub for a few moments in a circular motion. Lift the stone off the abrasive paper and look at the surface. If tiny scratch marks are evenly dispersed across the surface, the stone is flat. But, if only the ends of the stone show any signs of scratches, as is often the case, then the center of the stone is worn unevenly. To correct this problem and restore a flat surface to your stone, simply run the stone over the abrasive paper in a circular motion with the curved side down. To prevent clogging the surface of the stone, add a few drops of water periodically to help carry off the loose particles. This action will also clean the surface pores of the stone, which often become clogged with oil and tiny bits of steel from previous sharpening. Remember to oil the stone heavily after sanding.

In time, all bench stones will require a thorough cleaning. Clean the stone with a stiff fiber brush and kerosene until the surface has been restored, then resoak in mineral oil. If the surface of your bench stone should ever become glazed, clean with kerosene or lighter fluid and a stiff brush, or by rubbing the surface with coarse abrasive paper. Reoil the stone before use.

Abrasive Papers

During a sharpening task, it often is helpful to use some type of abrasive paper for preparing the edge of the tool prior to sharpening on a bench stone. Abrasive paper is also handy for removing rust on the surface of a tool and even for polishing. Very often a tool's edge can be quickly touched up between serious sharpening with abrasive paper as well. Part of the beauty of abrasive paper is that it is relatively inexpensive to use.

For our purposes, abrasive papers that are useful for sharpening or touch-ups to a cutting edge are composed of a strong paper or cloth backing and a mineral grain abrasive coated face. The grains of abrasive are most commonly emery (a natural material) and silicon carbide (a man-made abrasive). Abrasive paper is available in a wide range of abrasive grit sizes. Coarse (about 80 grit) paper is a fast-cutting abrasive that is suitable for removing metal or rust from the surface of a tool. At the other end of the spectrum, we find abrasive papers with high numbers (such as 300), which actually polish more than cut the surface. Papers in this group are generally referred to as *crocus cloth* and are very handy for touching up the edge of a tool.

The do-it-yourself sharpener should have a selection of abrasive papers in the home workshop. Although abrasive papers are not really suitable for heavy-duty sharpening tasks, they are quite handy for touching up an edge on a tool, for removing surface rust and for polishing.

Always use lubricating oil when working on a bench stone.

Using abrasive papers for light-duty sharpening is much easier to accomplish if you have some means of holding the paper flat and firmly as you work. One good way to hold the paper is to use a sanding block, either commercially made or homemade.

A simple but effective abrasive paper holder can be made easily in the home workshop from a piece of scrap lumber. The simplest type of holder is made from a piece of 1" × 4" lumber, approximately 8" long. A sheet of paper is fastened to this board with staples placed along the edges. This simple holder takes about two minutes to make and it will firmly hold abrasive paper while you touch up the edge of a tool. If you want to make the holder even more useful, fasten coarse emery cloth on one side and extra fine grit paper on the other side. You can also start off with a longer 1" × 4" board and cut out the shape of a handle on one end with a saber saw.

Other Sharpening Aids

Many sharpening aids, sharpening tools and hand-held sharpening machines are available for the do-it-yourself home sharpener. Some of these aids (such as a leather strop) have been around for centuries, while others, such as a battery-operated chain-saw sharpener, are relatively new. Let's look at a sampling of some of the more useful of these sharpening aids.

The barber's strop mentioned earlier is a very handy (although vanishing) sharpening aid. A strop will not sharpen a dull knife or razor but it will touch up a fairly sharp knife edge and make it razor sharp. You can make a similar strop from a smooth piece of leather. Fasten it to a board and give it a coating of lightweight oil — SAE 20, for example. This simple homemade strop is very useful for putting a finishing touch on a knife or tool that has already been sharpened on a bench stone. The proper way to use a strop is to push the tool away and along the strop, with the edge trailing. Never push the tool with the cutting edge forward. This will dull the tool and probably cut the strop as well.

A chef's steel is very useful for touching up knives in the kitchen and workshop before a cutting task. A chef's steel is simply a long tapered steel rod with tiny grooves (much like those on a single-cut file) running the entire length of the shaft. There are also grooveless and ceramic chef's steels available. It is important to keep in mind that a chef's steel does not have the ability to put an edge on a dull knife, but is used for touching up a knife that is almost sharp. A chef's steel can be used on a knife edge perhaps ten times before the knife must be reground and sharpened properly. A steel works by turning up and breaking off a very fine feather edge on the blade, thus generating a new cutting edge. A chef's steel is a good addition to any kitchen or workshop. When selecting a chef's steel, buy only one that has a guard in front of the handle. Since a knife is stroked toward the handle, you run the risk of cutting yourself without such a guard. There are also pocket steels, about the size of an ink pen, that are useful when a full-size chef's steel is not available.

Useful electrically powered sharpening machines have appeared in recent years. These include special handheld grinders and bench-mounted machines specifically designed for sharpening drill and router bits. Let's look at a few of these to see their value around the home workshop.

A twist drill bit sharpener is a handy little machine to have around the home workshop, especially if you use twist drill bits often. Generally speaking, there are two types of twist drill bit sharpeners available — those with an internal motor and those that require the use of an electric drill for power. Each has advantages and disadvantages. The self-contained twist drill bit sharpener offers convenience. Simply turn a switch and it is ready to sharpen twist drill bits of most sizes. On the negative side, the self-contained drill bit sharpener costs around forty dollars.

A twist drill bit sharpener that requires the use of your electric drill for operation is inexpensive, about half the price of the self-contained unit. This unit is also small enough to store easily in a standard drill case. About the only weak points about this unit are that it requires you to hook up your electric drill before you can use it, and each drill bit to be sharpened must be chucked into the drill before use. Although these tasks are not difficult, they do consume a bit of time and prevent you from using your drill for anything else at the time. In any event, either type of twist drill bit sharpener works well at restoring the tip of most standard size drill bits and is a worthwhile investment for the do-it-yourselfer.

If you do a lot of woodworking with a router, you should consider buying a special *router bit sharpening attachment*. This device, which clamps onto your router, securely holds any standard steel router bit while a special sharpening wheel spins. This sharpening wheel is chucked into the jaws of the router. The holding mechanism is fully adjustable so you can sharpen any size router bit. In addition, the sharpening wheel is a very hard man-made material that can sharpen both hard steel and carbide-tipped router bits. A router bit sharpening device, which is most commonly sold in kit form, is a very worthwhile investment for the home craftsman who does a lot of woodworking with a router.

A *belt sander* can also be used for some types of sharpening operations around the home workshop. Generally speaking, this electric sanding tool, of which there are two suitable types, is most effective when used to put a working edge on tools that do not require a razor-sharp edge — scissors and snips,

A sanding block made from 1″ × 4″ × 8″ lumber and covered with sandpaper and emery cloth is handy for light touch-up type sharpening.

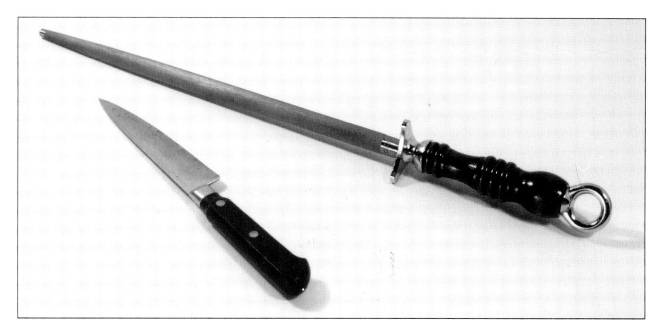

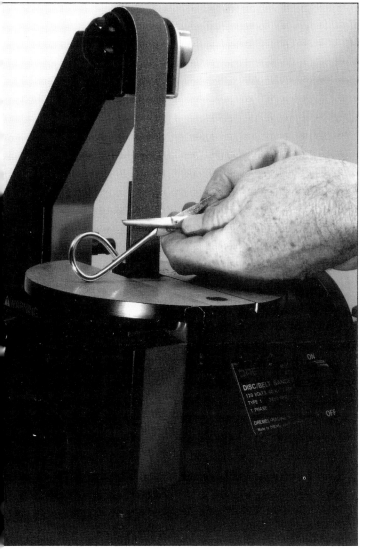

Chef's steel is handy in the workshop as well as the kitchen.

A vertical belt sander, such as this Dremel®, is handy for a variety of sharpening tasks.

for example. The two best types of belt sanders for this type of sharpening are a common handheld belt sander, and a stationary or bench-mounted type that uses an abrasive belt about 1″ wide. As a rule, the finer grit or grades of abrasive belts work best for most types of sharpening tasks.

The Dremel Moto-Tool® is another handy sharpening tool that can be used for power grinding small cutters such as those found on router bits. As a rule, the variable speed units are better for sharpening, as the speed can be regulated to suit a particular sharpening task. A wide variety of silicone carbide and diamond grit sharpening stones are also available to help sharpen a wide range of woodworking tools.

To be sure, other types of sharpening aids and tools are available. But, as a rule, almost all sharpening tasks can be accomplished with a file, stone or grinding wheel. In the following chapters I will mention other sharpening devices that can be useful for specific sharpening tasks.

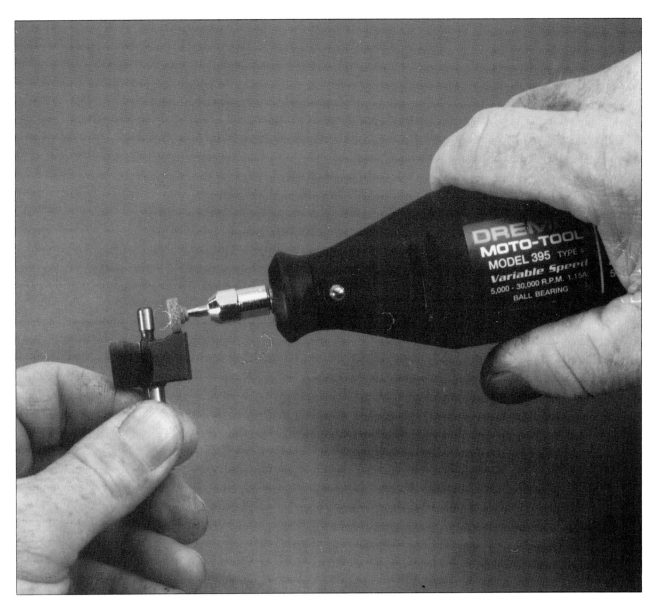

*Dremel Moto-Tool® is useful for many types of diffi-
cult sharpening projects.*

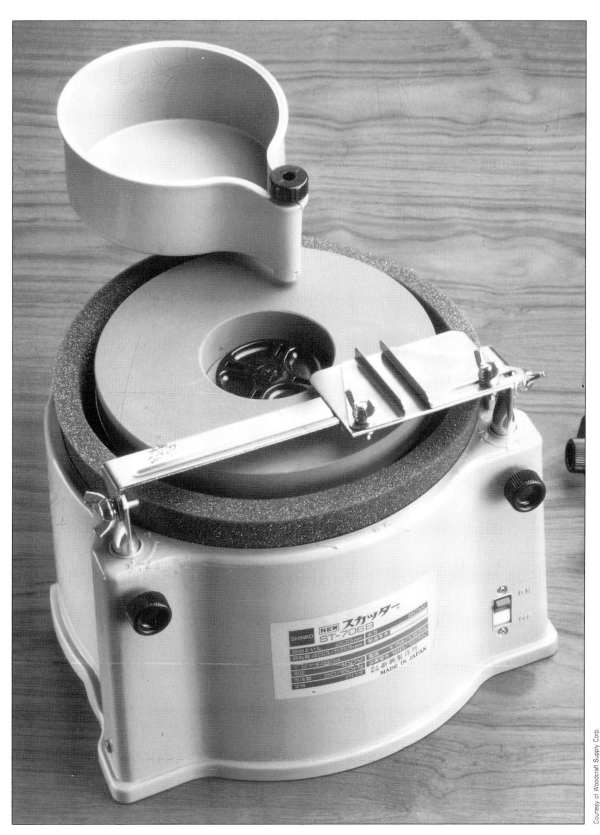

*Wet grinders run cool and therefore do not alter the
temper of tool steel.*

CHAPTER THREE
Sharpening Chisels

I t is no secret that a wood chisel works best when razor sharp. Oddly enough, whenever I inspect a fellow woodworker's chisel, I generally find it to be a little on the dull side. Even new, unused chisels are not as sharp as they should be to accomplish a task well. Another reason that most chisels are not in the best shape possible is the way in which they are stored. In this chapter I will cover how to recondition and sharpen woodworking chisels. I will also offer suggestions for keeping your chisels sharp

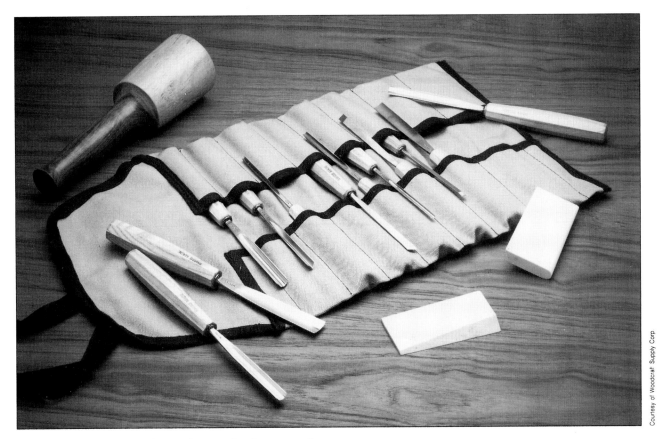

When well cared for and stored properly, sharp wood-working chisels are a joy to work with.

through proper storage practices.

Generally speaking, a wood chisel having a beveled cutting edge and a flat back is an easy tool to sharpen. After you have mastered chisel sharpening, it is a simple matter to sharpen other single-bevel-edged tools, such as plane blades and jointer knives. Chisel sharpening is done in three steps: inspecting, grinding, and sharpening on a stone. In some cases, only the last step is required to restore a woodworking chisel to top working condition.

Inspecting Chisels

The first step in the sharpening process of a wood chisel is to carefully look over the cutting edge to determine the amount of sharpening required. If the leading edge is nicked and/or corners rounded the chisel will require grinding to restore a flat edge and square corners. If, on the other hand, the cutting edge is simply dull, with no nicks present, then the chisel can be sharpened on a bench stone without grinding.

Often a chisel must be cleaned before a thorough inspection can take place. This is most easily accomplished by rubbing the shaft of the chisel with fine steel wool. Remove any rust and resin that may be on the surface of the tool. If the surface has become pitted or discolored, use crocus cloth (extremely fine grit) or emery cloth (fine grit) to restore the surface.

Lastly, check the handle of the chisel. Because a chisel is struck with a mallet or hammer during use, the handle can become damaged and should be repaired or replaced before use. If the blade is loose inside the handle, repair with woodworker's glue.

Grinding Chisels

The second step in the sharpening process for a wood chisel is to regrind the cutting edge. This is actually a two-step process that must (1) restore the

A nicked or chipped cutting edge requires grinding.

leading edge so that it is square and (2) restore the bevel. If your intention is to grind the edge to remove nicks, grind only to this depth.

For all but the most damaged chisels, a fine grit grinding wheel is best for restoring the edge of most tools. A fine grit grinding wheel will remove material quickly and the finished edge will not appear overly rough. If extensive damage has been sustained, a medium grit grinding wheel should be used initially, then switch to a fine grit wheel for finishing off the task.

The main point to keep in mind when grinding the edge of a chisel—or any steel tool, for that matter—is never to allow the tool to heat up to the point where the metal changes color. If the edge discolors quickly to a deep blue color, as it will if the tool is forced into the grinding wheel, it has been overheated. All of the discolored metal must then be ground away more carefully than previously so it does

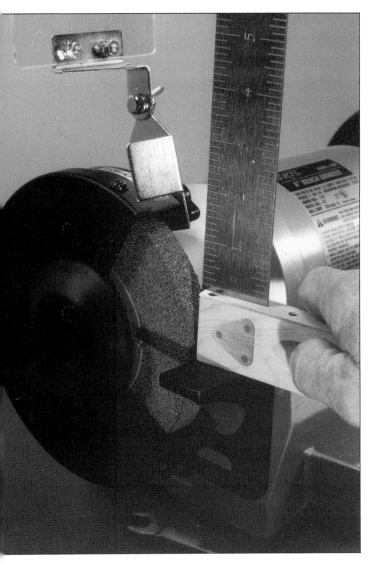

Adjust the grinder's tool rest to horizontal using a try square.

Wood Chisel Edge Bevel Angles

15° — Light carving

20° — Wood carving

25° — General-purpose bevel

30° — Mortise and deep cutting

Chisel edge bevel chart.

not become overheated again.

Before you begin grinding the leading edge of a chisel, adjust the tool rest on the bench grinder so that it is horizontal or 180° off the surface of the wheel. Use a try square or other suitable tool to make this important adjustment. Then place the damaged chisel on the tool rest with the bevel side up, and grind the cutting edge square to the sides of the chisel and back. Grind to the bottom of the nick. Keep the tool moving left to right so that the wear on the grinding wheel will be even and the chisel will not heat excessively. Do not grind any more off the edge than is necessary to remove the nick.

If the nick or nicks are deep, extensive grinding will be necessary to restore the edge. Dip the chisel into a container of water to keep it from heating up to the point where the temper of the metal is removed.

Once the edge of the chisel has been restored to square, the bevel must be reground. Begin by adjusting the tool rest for the desired bevel. The chart below lists the commonly used edge bevels for woodworking chisels. Use a protractor to make this adjustment and tighten the tool rest so that it remains rigid during use.

Grind the bevel by holding the chisel firmly on the tool rest and lightly pressing it into the spinning wheel. A ⅜″ (9 mm) bevel is suitable for most general types of woodworking.

After you have ground for a few moments — this grinding goes very quickly — remove the tool from the grinder and examine the bevel in progress. If the bevel is too short, you should adjust your technique by lowering the chisel handle, or by holding it up further on the wheel. If it is too long, you can raise the handle end or place it lower on the wheel. Keep in mind that a light touch will produce the kind of bevel you are after. Once again, dip the chisel in water to make certain that it is not becoming too hot to the touch.

Continue grinding until the edge is beveled

properly and a wire edge is produced on the back (flat) side of the chisel. This can be observed by looking carefully at the end of the chisel, or by drawing the flat side across the palm of your hand. If the flat side is smooth, it is an indication that the edge has not been turned properly. The turned edge will slightly scratch your hand when sharp. It will feel like a tiny wire on the back edge of the chisel.

Sharpening Chisels With a Bench Stone

The first step of stone sharpening, after the edge has been squared and the bevel established, is to flatten the back of the chisel. This is an essential task and should not be done casually. This step is necessary after a chisel has been ground, or prior to stone sharpening a chisel that simply needs touching up, or on a new, never before used chisel.

Courtesy of Woodcraft Supply Corp.

Use a bevel guide to check the bevel on your chisel during sharpening. This one works with both square and gouge chisels.

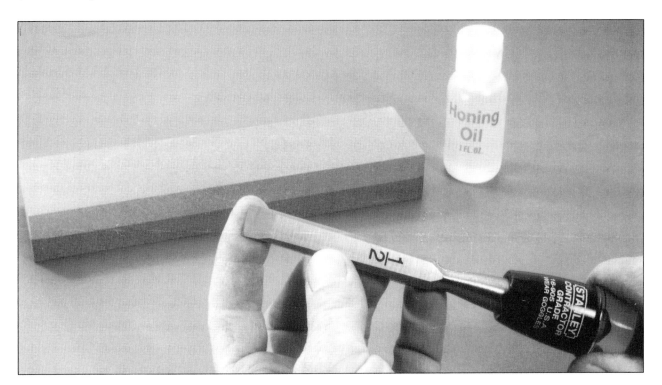

When ground properly, a tiny wire edge will form on the flat side of your chisel. You can feel this tiny wire with your finger pad.

Your intention is to make the back of the chisel perfectly flat and, in the process, slightly polish the back as well. Just how sharp you want the chisel to be is directly related to how flat the back of the chisel is. As a rule, you can use a bench grinder for this flattening, but never use a vertical grinder or abrasive belt. Many experts seem to concur that the best way to flatten and polish the back of a chisel is on a medium to fine bench stone.

Before you begin, check that the surface of the bench stone is itself flat. To check the flatness of the surface of a bench stone, lay it on a flat piece of 80 grit sandpaper and rub for a few moments in a circular motion. Lift the stone off the abrasive paper and look at the surface. If tiny scratch marks are evenly dispersed across the surface, the stone is flat. But if only the ends of the stone show any signs of scratches — a common problem with older, well-used bench stones — then the center of the stone is worn unevenly. To correct this problem and restore a flat surface to your stone, simply run the stone over the abrasive paper in a circular motion with the curved side down. To prevent clogging the surface of the stone, add a few drops of water periodically to help carry off the loose particles. This action will also clean the surface pores of the stone, which often become clogged with oil and tiny bits of steel from previous sharpening. Remember to oil the stone heavily after sanding.

Begin flattening and polishing the back of the chisel by making small circular strokes across the surface of the bench stone. Apply uniform pressure over the chisel as you work it over the surface. You should apply a few drops of honing oil to the surface of the stone before starting and add a few more drops if needed during the polishing.

Try to use the ends and corners of the stone as you work to flatten the back of the chisel. Use the middle of the stone later when you are sharpening the beveled edge of the chisel.

After the back of the chisel has been flattened and polished, you can turn your attention to the

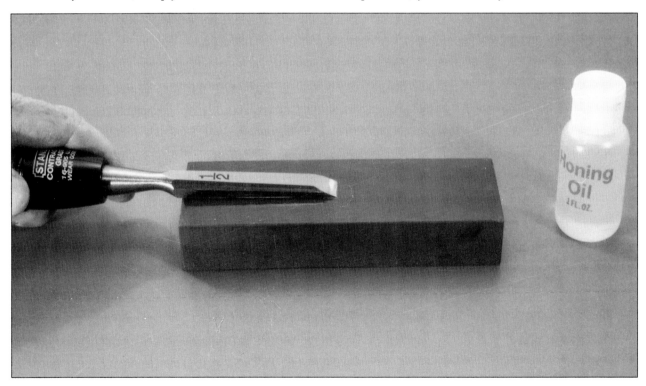

Flatten and polish the back of a chisel using a circular motion on an oiled whetstone.

bevel. A honing guide, available from many of the woodworking tool suppliers, will make this task easier to accomplish and give predictable results. This is especially true if you are relatively new to sharpening, where many find it difficult to hold the tool at the correct bevel angle consistently. In time, however, you may find that the use of a honing guide is unnecessary. Actually, honing the bevel of a chisel is easier than polishing the back, as there is generally less metal to be ground.

Begin honing the bevel by first applying a few drops of oil to the face of the stone. (Use a medium or fine grit stone.) Then hold the chisel at the angle of the bevel and apply pressure directly downward while moving the chisel straight forward, then backward. Make about six passes in this manner then turn the chisel over and hone the backside as well. Alternating the honing in this manner will make another burr form along the cutting edge. This is called the *honing burr* and, once it is developed, your chisel is almost sharpened.

Check the edge of the chisel after the bevel and back have been honed in the above manner about four times. Sometimes the honing burr will be visible, other times it must be felt with the pad of a finger. Once you see or feel this burr, use your finest stone to work both the back and bevel to remove the burr.

The last step in sharpening a chisel properly is to create a secondary bevel along the cutting edge. This takes only a few strokes with a fine grit stone but will add razor sharpness to the edge. The angle for the secondary bevel is not exact but simply a few degrees more than the primary bevel on the face of the chisel. It can, in fact, vary from 2° to 10°. As a rule, the steeper the secondary bevel the tougher the edge and the less likely the edge will chip. But, the more acute the secondary bevel the sharper the edge will be, which also means that the edge will dull more quickly during use.

To create the secondary bevel make a few light strokes on your finest stone. Don't forget to add a

A chisel bevel guide will help you make a perfect edge bevel.

few drops of oil before beginning. After a few strokes, feel the edge. If a burr has developed, stroke the flat and bevel sides of the chisel a few times to remove it. Now your wood chisel should be as sharp as possible, so you will want to test the edge.

Obviously the best way to test a woodworking chisel is on a piece of wood. The real test of chisel sharpness is on the end grain of wood. A sharp chisel will shave the end grain fibers like a razor with little or moderate effort.

Keeping a Chisel's Edge Sharp

Once you have taken the time to put a keen edge on your woodworking chisel, you will want to keep

Slip-on edge guards will protect your chisels from damage around the shop and during transport.

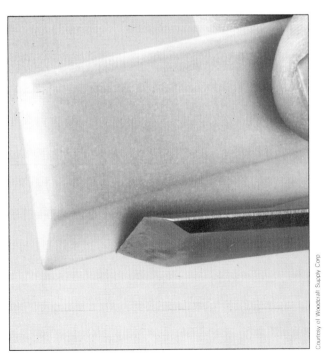

Form a secondary bevel with a few strokes of a fine grit stone.

that edge as long as possible without having to grind and resharpen too often.

To begin with, I always touch up the cutting edge of a chisel (reestablish the secondary bevel) before use, assuming that the edge has not been damaged. This operation takes only a few moments, but is worth the investment in time, as I can be certain that I will have a sharp tool to work with. Unless the chisel sustains some damage to the edge, I can usually touch up a chisel's edge four to six times before the tool requires regrinding.

Proper storage of a sharp chisel will greatly extend its working life. Store your woodworking chisels protected in the shop. A special rack or drawer is best. Carrying chisels away from the shop poses some additional problems as an unprotected edge can be easily chipped or otherwise damaged.

One solution is to purchase plastic slip-on guards to protect the cutting edges of your chisels. These come in a variety of standard sizes and are an effective way of keeping your woodworking chisels sharp while in transit or when not in use.

Another way to carry chisels away from the shop is in a canvas roll. Traveling carpenters of yesteryear carried their prize chisels in such a manner. Today, canvas chisel rolls can be purchased or made at home.

One last way of protecting a chisel from damage during storage or transport is to encase the metal shaft in a custom bamboo case. I have been using such a case for years and have never had a chisel edge nicked while so encased. My chisel sheath consists of a 9½″ piece of bamboo. One end of this tube contains the ring or node of the bamboo, and the other end is simply open to receive a ¾″ woodworking chisel. I have several wraps of tape around the case to hold it together. As I recall, the repair was necessary one day after dropping a hammer on top of the case with the chisel inside. As it turns out, bamboo is as strong as brass and the chisel was not harmed.

As you have seen in this chapter, sharpening a woodworking chisel is not difficult nor does it take

A bamboo chisel cover will protect your chisel from damage.

much time. A sharp chisel does the job faster and cleaner than a dull one, so it will be to your advantage to learn how to put an edge on this valuable woodworking tool. Then, store your woodworking chisels carefully so they will be ready for service when needed.

A canvas chisel roll is a good way to carry your chisels.

CHAPTER FOUR

Sharpening Plane Irons, Drawknives and Spokeshaves

It has been said that the plane is the aristocrat of woodworking tools. Of all the basic tools, the plane is probably the most misunderstood and complicated. When sharpened properly (which you will learn how to do in this chapter), a plane is a beautiful tool to work with. But when a plane is dull or not adjusted properly, it is a definite source of frustration. Drawknives and spokeshaves have blades similar to planes and are therefore covered in this chapter as well. But first, let's look at woodworking planes.

Although the blade of a typical bench plane is still commonly referred to as a plane "iron," modern

Woodworking planes are often called the "aristocrat" of hand woodworking tools.

Carefully inspect your plane iron bevel edge for chips or nicks. If any are present, the plane iron must be ground to remove them.

blades are actually made from high-carbon tool steel and hold an edge much longer than the old planes, which really did have blades made from iron. As a rule, plane irons are easier to sharpen if you have mastered sharpening woodworking chisels. Although the process is basically the same, there is more work involved simply by virtue of the size difference between the two.

A variety of woodworking planes are available to the modern woodworker. The list includes: smoothing planes, jack planes, fore/try planes, rabbet planes and block planes. Generally speaking, all of these are sharpened in the same manner, as they all have flat/beveled blades.

Sharpening a Plane Iron

Most experts will agree that there are six basic steps to sharpening a plane iron: (1) inspecting, (2) grinding the cutting edge to remove nicks or damage, (3)

flattening and polishing the back, (4) grinding a bevel, (5) honing, and (6) forming the secondary bevel. We will cover each of these steps in detail.

Inspecting

The first step in sharpening a plane iron is to remove it from the tool and carefully look it over. Your inspection will indicate the amount of work that will be required to restore a keen edge. If the edge has been damaged with nicks or gouges, it will require regrinding. The same treatment will be required if the corners are rounded. However, if the cutting edge is simply dull, with no damage, then the second step (grinding the cutting edge) can be skipped.

Grinding the Cutting Edge

A damaged cutting edge on a plane iron can be squared in a number of ways, depending of course on the extent of the damage. If, for example, small nicks are present, the iron can usually be touched up with a file, removing enough metal so that no damage is visible. On the other hand, if deep nicks or chips are present, the edge will require grinding to remove the damaged area.

Before you begin grinding the leading edge of a plane iron, adjust the tool rest on the bench grinder so that it is horizontal or 180° off the surface of the wheel. Use a try square or other suitable tool to make this important adjustment. Then place the damaged plane iron on the tool rest with the bevel side up, and grind the cutting edge square to the sides of the iron and back. Grind to the bottom of the nick or damaged area. Keep the tool moving left to right so that the wear on the grinding wheel will be even and the plane iron will not heat excessively. Do not grind any more off the edge than is necessary to remove the damaged area.

If the nicks or chips are deep, extensive grinding will be necessary to restore the edge. Dip the plane

Light nicks usually can be removed with a few strokes of a file.

iron into a container of water to keep it from heating up to the point where the temper of the metal is removed. Check the squareness of the edge with a try square often. Stop grinding when the edge is both flat and true.

You can take the sharpness off both corners of the leading edge of the plane iron if you plan on planing large flat surfaces, such as a tabletop. Do this with a bench stone after the plane iron has been perfectly squared.

Flattening and Polishing the Back·

The third step in the sharpening process for a plane iron is to work the back to flatten and polish this surface. Although this can be done on a grinding wheel, it is usually best to flatten and polish the back of a plane iron on a medium to fine grit bench stone.

Your intention is to make the back of the plane iron perfectly flat. This will also polish the back and make the plane iron cut better. Just how sharp you want the plane iron to be is directly related to how

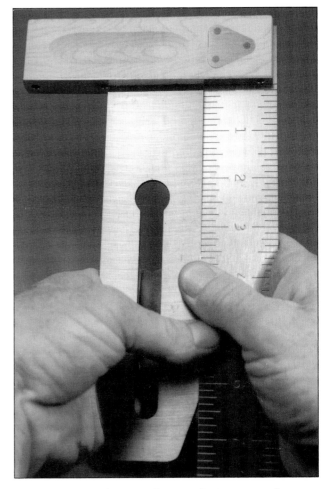

Check the squareness of your plane iron with a try square.

flat the back is.

Before you begin, check that the surface of the bench stone is itself flat. To check the flatness of the surface of a bench stone, lay it on a flat piece of 80 grit abrasive paper and rub for a few moments in a circular motion. Lift the stone and look at its surface. If tiny scratch marks are evenly dispersed across the surface, the stone is flat. But if only the ends of the stone show any signs of scratches, a common problem with older, well-used bench stones, then the center of the stone is worn unevenly.

To restore a flat surface to your stone, simply run the stone over the abrasive paper in a circular motion with the curved side down. To prevent clogging the surface of the stone, add water periodically to help carry off the loose abrasive.

Begin flattening and polishing the back of the plane iron by adding a few drops of honing oil to the stone and making circular strokes across the surface. Apply uniform pressure over the iron as you work.

Your intention is to make the back of the plane iron as flat as possible and, in the process, polish the back. You must remove all surface grinding marks (if you used a grinder initially) by using progressively finer abrasive grit stones. In the end, the back of your plane iron should have a mirror finish.

It should be noted that even new plane irons need to have the back of the iron polished in this manner to remove any marks that occurred during manufacture. Once this time-consuming task has been accomplished, however, you will find that

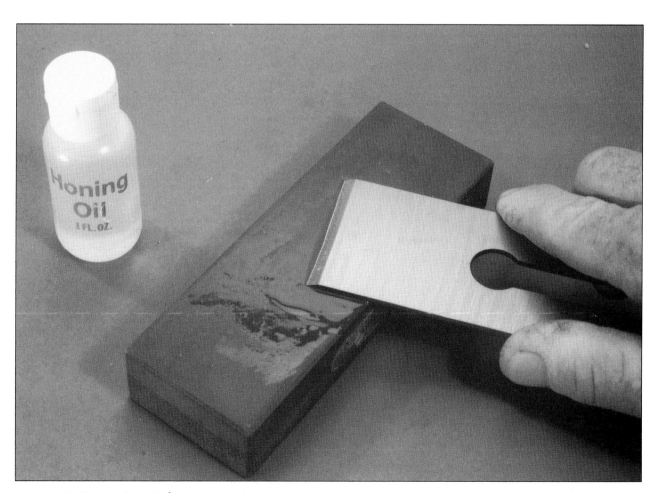

Flatten the back of a plane iron on a bench stone.
Be sure to use lubricant.

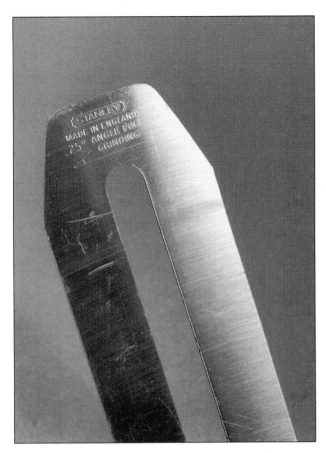

Tool marks on the flat side of a new plane iron should be polished out on a bench stone.

repolishing it will be a relatively simple and quick task.

Grinding the Bevel

Once the edge of the plane iron has been restored to square, and the back flattened and polished, the bevel must be reground. Begin by adjusting the tool rest for the desired bevel. As a rule, a bevel of 25° is used for planing softwoods and 30° is considered a general-purpose bevel. Use a protractor to help determine this adjustment and tighten the tool rest so that it remains rigid during use.

Grind the bevel by holding the plane iron firmly on the tool rest and lightly pressing it into the spinning wheel. A 3/16" (5 mm) bevel is suitable for most general types of woodworking.

After you have made a few passes, remove the plane iron from the grinder tool rest and examine the bevel in progress. If the bevel is too short, adjust your technique by lowering the plane iron or by holding it up further on the wheel. If it is too long, raise the handle end or place it lower on the wheel. Keep in mind that a light touch will produce the kind of bevel you are after. Once again, dip the plane iron in water to make certain that it is not becoming too hot to the touch.

Continue grinding until the edge is beveled properly and a wire edge is produced on the back (flat) side of the plane iron. This can be observed by looking carefully at the end of the iron, or by feeling the back with the pad of your thumb. If the flat side is smooth, the edge has not been ground correctly. A properly turned edge will feel as if there is a small wire along the edge.

Honing

After the back of the plane iron has been flattened and polished, and the front side rebeveled, the next step is to hone the bevel. A honing guide will make grinding the bevel easier unless you have a keen eye. In time however, you may find that the use of a honing guide is unnecessary. Honing the bevel of a plane iron is easy because the area to be worked is rather small — the beveled area.

Begin honing the bevel by first applying a few drops of oil to the face of the stone. (Use a medium or fine grit stone.) Hold the plane iron at the angle of the bevel and apply pressure directly downward while moving it straight forward, then backward. Make about six passes in this manner, then turn the plane iron over and hone the backside as well. After a few alternating passes, a burr will develop, indicating that the sharpening is proceeding correctly.

Check the edge of the plane iron after the bevel and back have been honed as described. Sometimes the honing burr will be visible; other times it must

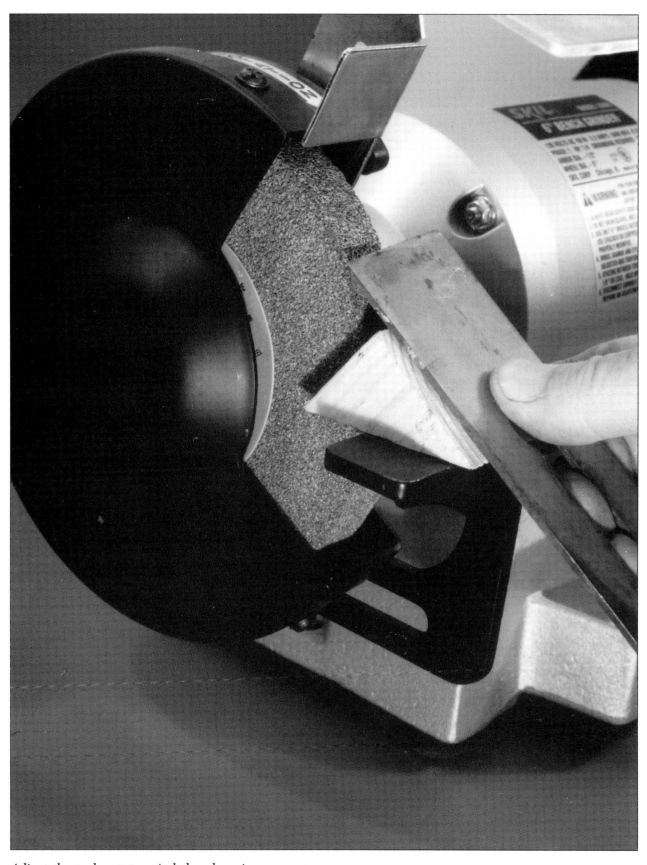

Adjust the tool rest to grind the plane iron square.

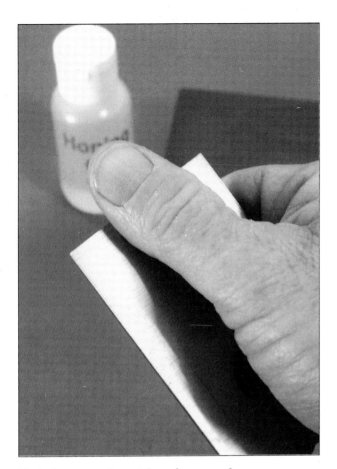

Feel the wire edge with a finger pad.

be felt with the pad of a finger. Once you see or feel this burr, use your finest stone to work both the back and bevel to remove the burr.

Forming the Secondary Bevel

The last step in sharpening a plane iron properly is to create a secondary bevel along the cutting edge. This goes quickly on a fine grit stone and will add extra keenness to the edge. The angle for the secondary bevel is not exact but simply about 5° more than the primary bevel on the face of the plane iron. Thus if your primary bevel is 25°, the secondary bevel will be 30°.

To create the secondary bevel, make a few light strokes on your finest stone. Don't forget to add a few drops of oil before beginning. After a few strokes, feel the edge. If a burr has developed, stroke the

back and bevel sides of the plane iron alternately to remove it.

Keeping a Plane Iron Sharp

After you have spent the time to properly sharpen a woodworking chisel, you will want to keep it razor sharp and ready for the next time it is needed. The first thing to do is to loosen the lever and draw the plane iron up into the mouth opening of the base so the iron is not exposed. Then lock the iron in place. This small act will do much to prevent damage to the plane iron cutting edge. When you need to use the plane, simply loosen the lever, lower the plane iron into the desired working position and lock it in place.

Plane iron edge bevel tool will help you to make a perfect beveled edge on a bench stone.

A drawknife is handy for peeling bark and shaving green wood.

Draw a plane iron up into the housing when not in use to protect the sharp edge from damage.

During use it is possible to damage a woodworking plane simply by placing it base down on the workbench. Always lay a plane on its side when not in use.

Finally, store your plane out of harm's way. This can be on a shelf, in a special wooden box or in a cabinet.

A high-quality woodworking plane should provide a lifetime of working pleasure providing it is sharpened and used properly. Storing your fine tool in a safe place will ensure that the tool is always ready for service when needed.

Sharpening a Drawknife

Although it is not commonly used by the average home woodworker, a *drawknife* is quite handy for some roughing work on timber and lumber prior to

construction. When building with logs, for example, a drawknife is indispensable for peeling the bark off green or semidry timber. As a rule, a drawknife is used for rough work and is followed by a plane or other suitable finishing tool. A drawknife is sometimes referred to as a *drawshave*.

A drawknife is used by angling it on the work to control the cut depth, and then pulling it toward you. It is best to cut only with the grain to more easily control depth of cut. A drawknife can be used on convex and concave surfaces as well as flat surfaces. On convex surfaces, work with the bevel on top of the tool. On concave and flat surfaces, face the bevel down into the work.

Drawknives are fairly simple to sharpen, as the blade is flat on one side and beveled on the other, much like a plane iron, only longer (10″ to 13″ long). Begin with a careful inspection of the cutting edge. Nicks and chips must, of course, be removed by grinding. Sometimes the two handles of a drawknife will interfere by coming in contact with some part of the grinder. Check this out before attempting to grind. If you cannot grind the entire edge unobstructed, you must clean up the edge with a flat file.

Alternately stone the bevel and flat sides of a drawknife.

Work with the drawknife clamped into a bench vise.

If you can work on a bench grinder, adjust the tool rest to the horizontal position. Hold the drawknife with the bevel up during grinding. Grind only enough metal to remove the damage. Stop often and check the squareness of the blade with a square. As with all grinding, keep the tool moving to prevent excess heat buildup. Since a drawknife blade is long, it is not possible to dip it in water to keep it cool. Instead, use a plant atomizer filled with water to spray the blade.

After the edge of the drawknife has been cleaned of blemishes, you must next regrind the bevel. For most purposes a 30° bevel is best. Adjust the tool rest to this angle and carefully regrind the bevel. Keep the drawknife moving to prevent heat buildup and strive to keep the leading edge square.

After the bevel edge of the drawknife has been ground, use a bench stone to further sharpen the tool. Work alternately on back (flat side) and bevel side to produce a wire edge. Carefully feel the edge

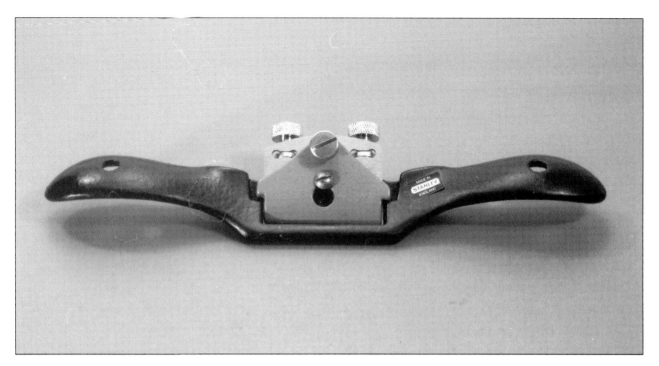

with a pad of a finger and continue until the wire is removed. As a rule, this concludes sharpening of a drawknife blade. A secondary bevel is not generally added to the edge of this tool.

It is important to protect the edge of a drawknife when not in use. I have found the best way to do this is to cover the cutting edge with a length of

Spokeshave.

garden hose that has been split down the middle. Simply cut the hose to size, split it with a razor knife, and attach over the cutting edge of the drawknife.

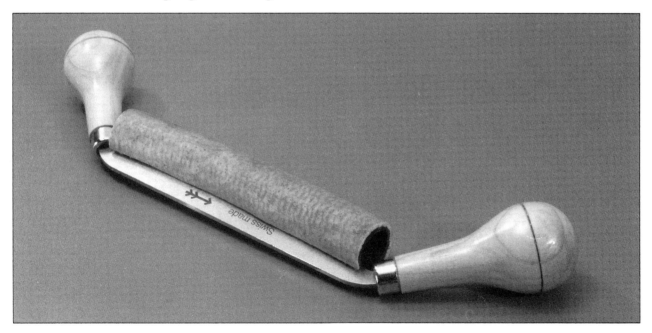

A split length of garden hose makes a good edge protector for a drawknife.

A spokeshave blade is very similar to a plane iron, only much shorter.

Sharpening a Spokeshave

The *spokeshave* can best be described as a kind of two-handled plane with a very short bottom and a wide throat. Its greatest use is in smoothing irregular or curved surfaces. Both straight- and curved-blade models are available. A spokeshave can be adjusted for depth of cut as well as angle of cut. The latter adjustment is made by adjusting either of the two knobs on the top of the unit.

To use a spokeshave, you hold one handle in each hand and place it on the work. Try to keep your thumbs on the back edges of the handle; this gives the best control. Push the spokeshave away from you just as you would a plane, and stop when the grain direction changes in a curve — usually about midway, but this can differ depending on the type and shape of the wooden material you are working on. Working with the grain in this manner helps prevent splits from tearing away from the work. A spokeshave can also be pulled toward you, providing

you are pulling with the grain of the wood.

The blade of a spokeshave is almost exactly like a plane iron, only much shorter, and is therefore sharpened in the same manner. Begin by removing the blade from the tool and carefully examine the cutting edge. If damage is apparent, the blade must be reground. If no damage is present, the edge can be sharpened with a bench stone.

When repairing a damaged spokeshave blade, use either a bench grinder or a flat file. The amount of damage will dictate the proper approach. Minor damage can easily be removed with a flat file; more extensive damage will require grinding.

Assuming a damaged edge, begin by removing metal (either by filing or grinding) until the damage is gone. Work carefully to keep the edge square, stopping often to check this area with a square. Remove only enough material to eliminate the damaged area and do not allow the spokeshave blade to become hot. As a rule, unless the damage is extensive, a few passes with a file or grinding wheel should be all that is required to restore a flat, true edge.

Next grind a bevel of 30°. Adjust the tool rest on the bench grinder to this angle and grind with the bevel down. Once again, do not allow the metal to heat up, as this will destroy the temper of the metal. After regrinding the bevel, work the blade alternately on a bench stone to develop a wire edge. You can accomplish the sharpening either freehand or with the aid of a honing guide.

Before reassembling the blade into the spokeshave, clean up the face of the tool to remove any rust, surface discoloration or burrs. Oil the adjusting screws lightly to make them operate properly as well.

When it is not in use, adjust the spokeshave blade so that it is not exposed during storage. Then, before use, adjust the tool for the task at hand.

CHAPTER FIVE

Sharpening Knives and Carving Tools

A dull knife is one of the most useless and frustrating tools in the kitchen, field or workshop. Since you cannot control the cutting action of a dull knife, you are just as likely to cut yourself as what you are working on, and the cut you will receive will actually be worse than a cut from a sharp knife. The only type of knife you should ever use is a sharp one. By the end of this chapter, you will know how to go about putting a keen edge on any knife or carving tool.

Sharpening Knives

Knife sharpening is not difficult, but many people make it so for some unknown reason. If a blade has not been damaged and you are not trying to change the basic design or bevel of the cutting edge, then it should only be a matter of minutes before you can put a decent working edge on almost any knife. In addition, there are a variety of sharpening devices that can make knife sharpening quick and simple.

Before we get into a discussion about how to sharpen a knife, we need first to take a brief look at the various types of cutting edges that are in common use. Any knife you might pick up will have one of four possible edges: cannel, hollow, concave or V-grind. Let's look at each of these and see what particular purpose each has been developed for.

Cutting Edges

The *cannel* edge or grind on a knife edge produces a strong cutting tool that can be used for heavy-duty cutting. A good example of an effective use of this edge design is a meat cleaver. Since this tool requires a blade with plenty of metal behind the cutting edge for chopping through bones in a manner similar to an ax, the cannel edge is the best choice.

The *hollow* or *hollow ground* cutting edge is a popular grind for general-purpose cutting and is probably the most common type of edge on pocketknives and other types of knives. Because of the wide bevel, this edge is easy to work with on most types of materials.

The *concave* edge design, some people feel, is even better for carving than the hollow ground blade, and is therefore used on many fine wood-carving tools. A concave edge design allows for very thin slices of material to be removed precisely. This edge is also most useful for knives used in the kitchen.

The V-*grind* provides a sturdy cutting edge and is very common on butcher knives and general-purpose kitchen knives. Although it does not stand up to continued use, it can be quickly sharpened with a butcher's steel prior to use.

These four blade bevels are considered the standards in the knife industry, but a knife blade may in fact be a combination of any two. For example, the typical pocketknife blade is basically a V-grind design

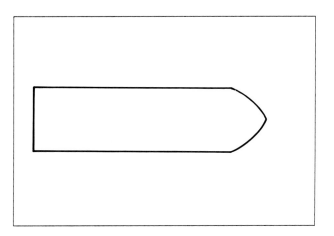

Cannel edge.

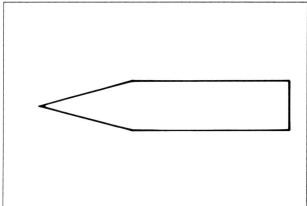

Concave edge.

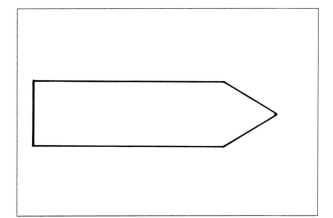

Hollow or hollow ground edge.

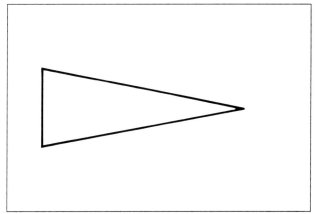

V-Grind edge.

but the cutting edge will, in most cases, be hollow ground. This approach to edge sharpening leaves enough metal behind the cutting edge to give strength and durability to the blade.

There are a number of different approaches to sharpening a knife, and this is where most people become confused. After all, there are hundreds of different machines, gadgets and sharpening aids on the market in addition to the basic tools for knife sharpening—files, steels, stones (of which there are many types) and bench grinders. In an effort to take as much confusion as possible out of sharpening a knife blade, we will for the most part discuss knife sharpening with the most basic sharpening equipment. This will give you a solid understanding of what is really involved. At the end of this chapter

we will also look at some of the sharpening aids available and explain how the most useful work.

Using the Bench Grinder

As a rule, the only time a bench grinder should be used on a knife blade is when the blade has been damaged—either nicked or broken at the tip. The heat generation of the average bench grinder will take the temper out of a knife blade in seconds, so you must always be careful not to let the blade get too hot during the grinding. Keep a container of water close by while working, and dip the blade often to cool. You should use a very light touch. In other words, don't force the grinding or try to remove too much material at one time.

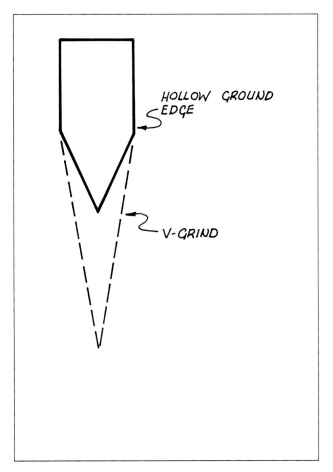

Hollow ground vs. V-grind edge.

Some bench grinders do not develop much heat as a result of being cooled by water during the grinding process. If you do much knife and tool sharpening, a cool-running bench grinder might be a good investment for your workshop.

When working on a conventional bench grinder, begin by adjusting the tool rest so that when the knife blade is placed there, the wheel will grind off at a perfect 90° angle. Grind the edge of the knife in this manner, keeping the blade moving constantly so that flat spots do not develop along the edge. Grind the blade only long enough for the nicks to disappear. If the damage is slight, this may take only one or two passes along the blade. If the damage is significant, however, you will be required to make several passes to remove the damaged area. In this case, stop often and dip the blade into the container of water. If the point of the knife has been damaged,

the same technique should be used to reestablish the curve and point. In no case should the blade be allowed to become red or white hot.

After the damaged area has been ground away, next readjust the tool rest to the proper bevel angle of the blade. Use the chart on page 50 as a general guideline, and a protractor to adjust the tool rest properly. Some do-it-yourselfers like to grind the bevel freehand, but this is possible only if you have a good eye and work very carefully. In any event, grind the edge bevel first on one side of the blade, then flip it over and grind the same bevel on the other side of the blade edge. When grinding, look for a fine wire edge, which will develop when the bevel has been ground properly. The next step is to finish off the sharpening on a bench stone. Once again, when grinding, keep the blade cool by frequent dipping in water, never allowing it to become too hot to touch.

Using Files

Another technique that poses almost no danger to the temper of the knife steel can be used to repair a damaged knife blade; it involves the use of a flat file. Begin by clamping the knife blade in a bench vise so that it is held securely level and at a comfortable working height. Next take the file and, holding its flat side perpendicular to the damaged knife edge, stroke the blade to remove the damage. Begin filing well behind the nick, and with a long stroke pass over the area and beyond. The strokes of the file should be long, smooth and even. The reason for beginning and ending the filing before and after the damaged area is so that you will be able to maintain the original contour of the blade, while at the same time repairing the damage. As you file, you will notice that the edge of the blade will become flat and much wider than when you started—how wide, of course, depends on the extent of the damage.

After the damage has been repaired, you must

Bevel Angles for Knives and Carving Tools

11° — Most narrow bevel; razor-sharp edge for X-Acto blades, woodcarving tools and speciality tools. This edge dulls quickly and must be resharpened often.

15° — Superior sharpness for butcher knives, fine carving tools and speciality knives.

19° — Best for kitchen cutlery.

22° — Wide bevel for a more durable working edge. Ideal for pocket knives, folding and fixed blade hunting knives and serrated knives.

25° — Widest bevel with longest lasting edge. For all utility cutlery.

Knife edge bevel angle chart.

rebevel the edge. This can be done with a file or stone. If the area is very thick (over 0.005"), you will have a lot of metal to bevel and will probably be better off using the file for most of the work. However, if the nick was not too deep, you did not have to remove too much metal; therefore the beveling and sharpening can be accomplished on a coarse bench stone.

Using the Bench Stone

It is probably safe to say that the most common tool for sharpening a knife is a stone. It is also true that most do-it-yourselfers do not use a sharpening stone correctly. By the end of this section you will have a

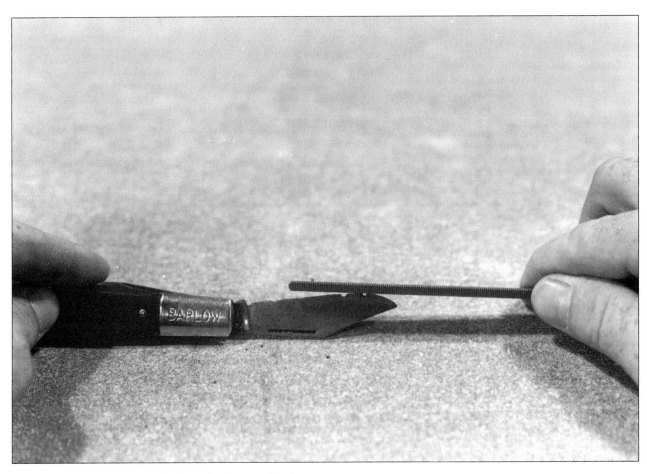

Use a flat file to remove light nicks from a knife edge.

better understanding of the process.

Probably the handiest stone to have around the home workshop is a combination stone. One side will be coarse (around 100 grit size) and the other side will be fine (around 600 grit size). Stones of this variety come in several sizes and range in price from around eight dollars for a pocket version to more than twenty-five dollars for a large bench model. Most combination stones are man-made, so you can be fairly certain as to uniformity.

A good combination stone will enable you to put a keen edge on almost any knife you come across, so it is a good investment. Since it can also be used for sharpening a number of other woodworking tools, such as a wood chisel, a combination bench stone is handy around the home workshop.

To sharpen a knife, begin by placing the stone,

coarse side up, on the edge of a table or bench. Next, add a few drops of honing oil to the surface. Use a special oil designed for the purpose or a lightweight oil or kerosene. Then, holding the knife behind the hilt, begin passing the blade over the stone. The cutting edge of the blade can either be leading or trailing—there are many theories here—but most important, the blade should be held at a consistent angle to form the edge bevel. I have found that the best way to sharpen a knife blade is to push it over the stone with the cutting edge leading—just as if I were shaving a fine layer off the top of the stone. Probably the best bevel angle for a general-purpose cutting edge is around 15° off the stone.

For all but the dullest or recently ground knives, no more than twenty strokes per side should be required to develop a 15° bevel. The procedure is to

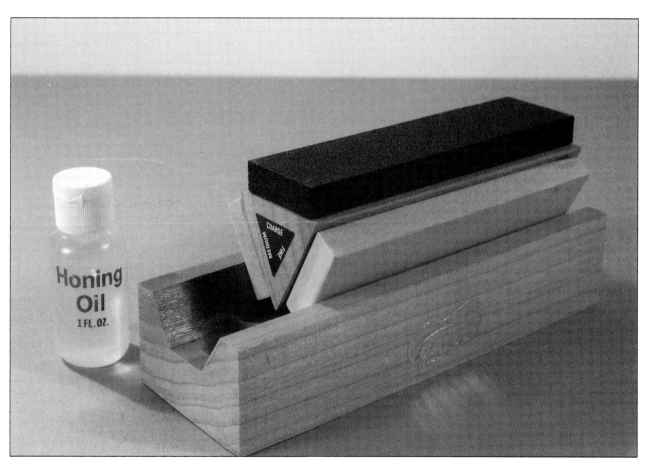

This three-sided combination stone is handy for a variety of sharpening tasks.

make one pass, then turn the blade over and go back over the stone to complete one pass. Although it is relatively easy to hold the blade at a 15° angle for the straight part of the cutting edge, as you near the tip of the knife, you must lift up slightly while at the same time developing the bevel around the point. Sometimes, especially on long knives, it is best to sharpen the blade in stages—first the straight part of the blade, then the curved tip section.

If you sharpen the blade only on the coarse side of the combination stone, you should develop a very good cutting edge that will be suitable for a variety of cutting tasks. But you may want the knife sharper for a specific task, such as whittling or carving. If this is the case, after you have achieved a fairly sharp cutting edge using the coarse side of the stone, flip the stone over, apply a few drops of oil, and begin resharpening the blade in the same manner. After about twenty passes you should have an almost razor-sharp edge on the knife.

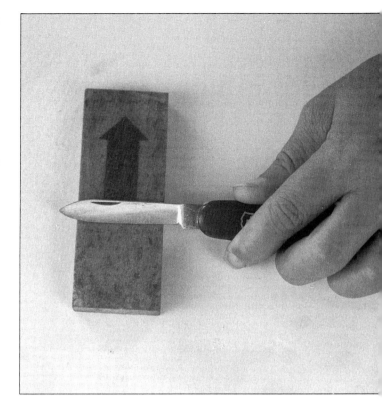

Maintain the correct edge bevel when sharpening a knife.

Troubleshooting

Problems in sharpening a knife can be caused by several factors. First, you may be holding the knife at the wrong angle. Remember that an angle of about 15° will give a good general-purpose cutting edge, but you must hold this blade angle consistently throughout the sharpening stroke—on both sides of the blade. This is a technique that is developed over time and only with concentration. Once you develop a knack for holding a consistent angle, 99 percent of your sharpening problems will be solved.

Another possible cause of problems when sharpening is a stone that is not flat. With time, all stones will develop a slight indented curve. This is a result of the nature of the work that sharpening stones are called upon to do, and is quite normal. Nevertheless, a bellied stone is difficult to sharpen on, so you should make the surface flat by sanding before using the stone for a sharpening task. In some extreme cases it is best to simply purchase a new combination stone rather than try to flatten a well-used stone.

To check the flatness of the surface of a bench stone—and *always* suspect old stones of being bellied—lay it on a flat piece of 80 grit sandpaper and rub for a few moments in a circular motion. Lift the stone off the abrasive paper and look at the surface of the stone. If tiny scratch marks are evenly dispersed across the surface, the stone is flat. But, as is often the case, if only the ends of the stone show any signs of scratches, then the center of the stone is worn unevenly. To correct this problem and restore a flat surface to your stone, simply run the stone over the abrasive paper in a circular motion with the curved side down. To prevent clogging the surface of the stone, add a few drops of water periodically to help carry off the loose particles. This action will also clean the surface pores of the stone, which often become clogged with oil and tiny bits of steel from previous sharpening. Remember to oil the stone heavily after sanding.

Using a Butcher's Steel

One of the handiest sharpening aids to have in the kitchen is a steel sharpening rod, and it makes good sense to have one around the workshop as well for touching up a slightly dull carving or general-purpose knife. There are several types on the market. Some are made from a ribbed steel rod, some are fairly smooth, and still others are made from ceramic or man-made stone. In any case, they all work in the same manner and are very useful for quickly restoring the edge on most knives. If you watch a professional butcher or food server, you will probably notice that he gives a few swipes of his knife to a steel before cutting. You will want to do the same if you have a cutting task at hand that requires a razor-sharp edge.

To use a *butcher's steel*, begin by holding it in your left hand with the knife to be sharpened in your right (assuming that you are right handed, southpaws make suitable adjustments), cutting edge downward. Next, begin making a pass down along the steel by starting at the tip of the steel with the leading edge of the knife. As you swipe down the steel, pull the knife toward you so that the entire edge of the blade passes over the steel along the way. As you near the end of the stroke, bend your wrist so that the tip or point area along the front of the knife blade passes over the steel as well. Give one stroke to one side of the blade, then make a pass with the other side of the blade touching the steel. During sharpening, you must hold the knife so that it is at an approximate angle of 18° throughout the entire stroke. In most cases, five or six passes per side should develop a razorlike edge on the blade.

If you are not able to develop a sharp edge on a knife with a butcher's steel, you may be holding

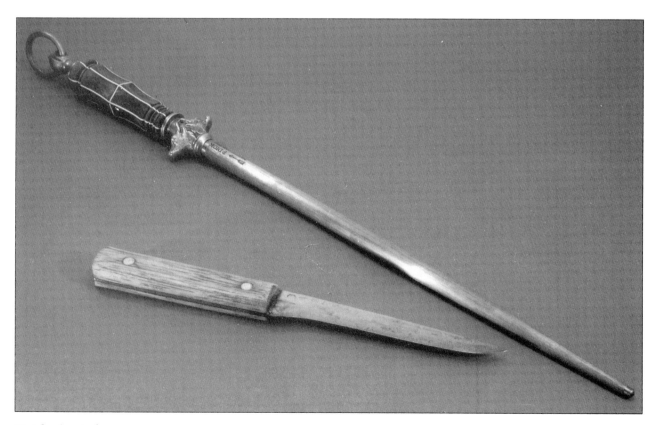

Butcher's steel.

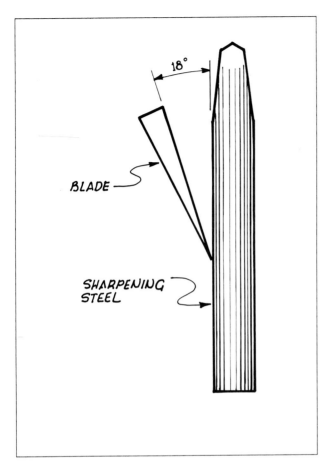

Strive to maintain an 18° bevel when using a butcher's steel.

the knife blade at the wrong angle. Keep in mind the fact that an angle of about 18° will help to produce the keenest edge. Another possibility for failure of a butcher's steel is clogged grooves along the shaft of the steel. As a knife is sharpened, microscopic pieces of steel are worn away and held in the grooves of the steel. In addition, a butcher's steel can become magnetized, as most do over time, and this action will also hold ground metal on the surface. To clean up a used butcher's steel, wipe it with a cloth that has been dampened in vegetable oil. You will be amazed at how much material will come off with just a few wipes. Then wipe the steel again with a dry cloth to remove the excess oil on the shaft. The sharpening ability of any butcher's steel will be greatly enhanced by this treatment.

Knife Sharpening Aids

There are probably more gadgets, gizmos and other so-called knife sharpeners than types of natural sharpening stones. While researching this book I discovered quite a few and must admit that some of these devices will help you to sharpen a knife, even if the user has never been able to sharpen a knife in the past. In just about every case, however, the device sharpens largely as a result of holding the knife blade at a consistent angle, or forces the user to hold a knife at a predetermined angle, most commonly about 15°. Since this is probably the most difficult part of sharpening for the beginner, such a sharpening aid should work for anyone. But if you can hold this angle freehand, you can usually do a better sharpening job with just a combination stone.

One of the simplest sharpening devices is simply a plastic disk with a round Carborundum stone in the center. In use a knife blade is drawn through the disk, with the side of the blade on a guide and the cutting edge on the stone. First one side of the blade is pulled through two or three times, then it is switched for the same treatment on the other side of the blade. This device is handy in the kitchen and workshop for restoring a keen edge quickly to an

Angle	Typical Use
11°	Most narrow bevel; razor-sharp edge for X-Acto blades, woodcarving instruments and specialty tools. This angle requires frequent sharpening as it dulls quickly.
15°	Superior sharpness; used for fillet, boning and other thin, specialty blades.
19°	Ideal for kitchen cutlery.
22°	A wider bevel; more durable edge. For pocketknives, fixed and folding hunting knives and serrated knife blades.
25°	Widest bevel; longest lasting edge. For all utility cutlery, carpet, linoleum and electrician's knives.

These sharpening rods make it easy to get the right edge bevel.

undamaged knife blade. I have found that using this device under running tap water does a better job of sharpening rather than attempting the task dry.

A popular addition to most electric can openers is a knife sharpener, usually on the rear of the unit. These tiny sharpeners are handy for general sharpening. A sharpener of this type, however, will not sharpen a knife forever. In time, the blade will require edge restoration on a combination bench stone.

Another knife sharpening system consists of two ceramic or man-made stone rods, either triangular or cylindrical. The rods are held in a **V** shape on some type of wooden or plastic base. These sharpeners work nicely and are popular for that reason. The theory behind these sharpeners is that the 15° angle is maintained as you push the knife blade downward along the shaft, much the same as a butcher's steel.

Such a sharpening device will put an almost razor-sharp edge on any undamaged knife blade, so it is a worthwhile investment for the workshop.

One other sharpening aid that I found worthwhile is the GATCO sharpening system. The basic kit contains three special sharpening stones (coarse, medium and fine grit), each mounted in finger-protecting plastic holders. Each stone is color coded and has a sliding rod guide that is used in conjunction with the unique knife clamp/angle guide. In addition, the kit comes with a plastic bottle of honing oil all packaged in a carrying case that contains directions for use inside the lid. GATCO also offers a "professional" sharpening system that contains two

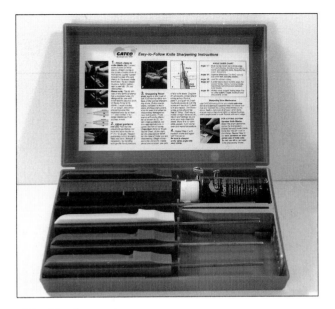

GATCO sharpening system.

additional stones—one very coarse and another for sharpening serrated knives and scissors.

The GATCO sharpening system is very simple to use, in large part because of the knife clamp/angle guide. Five angle positions can be used to put a variety of precise edges on any knife. The angles and their uses are explained in the table.

To use the GATCO sharpening system begin by attaching the clamp to the knife blade. Simply attach the clamp to the spine of the knife at midpoint and lightly tighten the forward screw. Next lock the blade in place by turning the rear screw. This can be accomplished with finger pressure and does not require a screwdriver.

Then select the coarse sharpening stone and pull

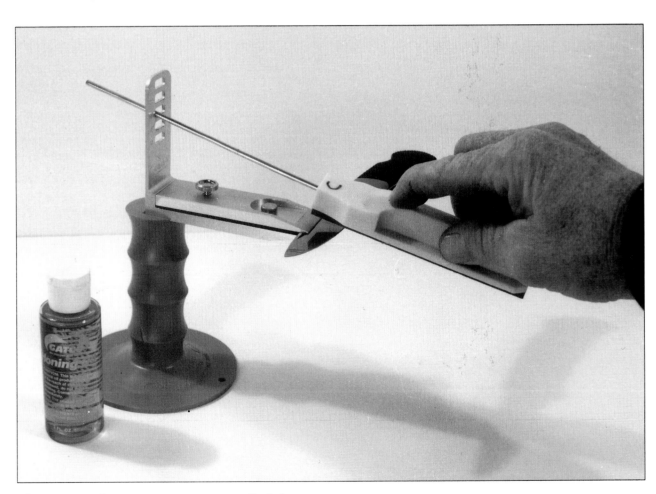

The GATCO sharpening system can really help you sharpen knives and a variety of other tools around the home and workshop.

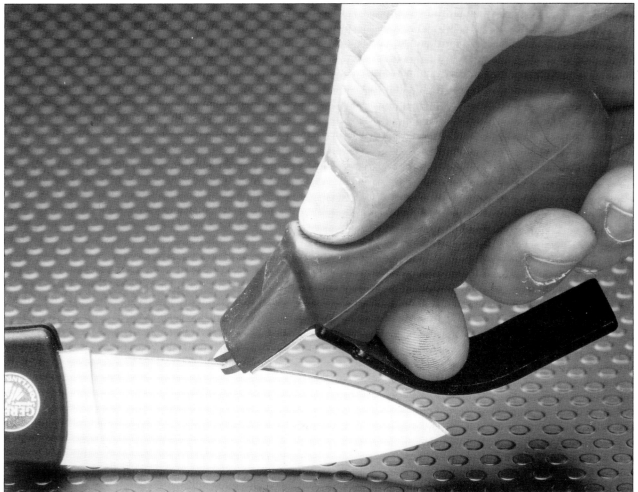

the guide rod out of the holder to a length of about 7″. Apply a thin coat of honing oil to the face of the stone and insert the guide rod into the appropriate angle guide hole, using the table on page 54. Next, beginning at the hilt of the knife, push the stone — with guide rod in the desired angle hole — straight forward. At the end of the stroke, lift the stone, pull rearward and repeat the process while working in stages toward the tip of the blade.

After the first side of the blade has been so sharpened with the coarse stone, remove the sharpening stone and guide rod, turn the clamp over and reinsert the guide rod into the same angle hole. Repeat the sharpening on the other side of the blade. Once both sides of the blade have been sharpened with the coarse stone, repeat the process using the

There are many ways to touch up a knife edge.

medium grit stone, and finish off the sharpening with the fine grit stone.

I have found that any knife blade can be sharpened with the GATCO sharpening system in just a few minutes. Even nicked blades can be repaired with care using the coarse stone. This sharpening system is a worthwhile addition to any workshop as it will help you to quickly sharpen any knife.

To be sure, there are a variety of gadgets to help you put a keen edge on any knife or carving tool, but once you have a mastery of sharpening, you can sharpen with a benchstone. Then you may want to use sharpening gadgets to save time.

CHAPTER SIX

Sharpening Lathe Knives and Turning Tools

Woodworking lathes are growing in popularity in home shops, particularly for furniture-building projects. The woodworking lathe has not changed in principle since it was invented in ancient Egypt. It is still a machine that turns a workpiece at a controlled speed while sharp tools are pressed against it, shaping it symmetrically. Obviously, electric motors have replaced foot power and high-tech metals are used for various components and tools, but the underlying principle remains the same.

A few basic tools are commonly used on a woodworking lathe, and with these almost any turning

project can be accomplished, from table legs to wooden bowls. To be sure, it takes time to learn the proper techniques. It is equally important to keep wood-turning tools sharp for predictable results.

Wood-turning tools, because they are used continuously, will require sharpening more often than most other types of woodworking tools. This is largely because wood is being removed quickly and this can wear out even the sharpest edges.

Almost any wood-turning project can be accomplished with one or more of six basic turning tools. These are grouped into two categories: shearing (cutting) tools and scraping tools.

Shearing Tools

Generally speaking, shearing tools are designed to slice away the wood in the form of sharply cut shavings, very much as skin is peeled from an apple. The two tools in this category are the *gouge* and the *skew*. Because these two tools are called upon to do an enormous amount of material removal, they are best when not sharpened too keenly, as super sharp edges would dull too quickly. Shearing tools, however, are honed after grinding, but a secondary bevel is not formed on the cutting edge.

A gouge is the most versatile of the wood turning tools for the woodworking lathe. As a rule, the gouge is the only chisel used to remove material when you're rough shaping. After you have mastered the technique, you will find that this is most quickly accomplished with a shearing action, holding the tool on its side and moving it parallel to the work. Start the roughing cut along the length of the work and not at one end.

The skew is most often used in a scraping action. It is useful for making tapers, squaring stock ends

◄ *A wood lathe is popular in many do-it-yourself woodworking shops.*

and so forth. It is also useful for smoothing down cylinders, but this requires a shearing (moving from side to side, while removing material) action and a great deal of practice. The skew can also be used to cut stock to length.

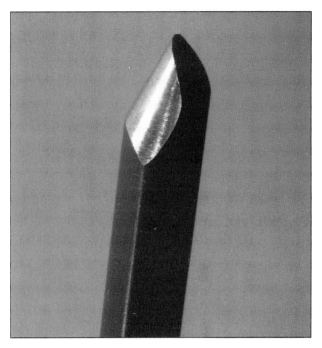

Gouge.

Skew.

Scraping Tools

Scraping tools are not designed to cut or slice through wood as shearing tools are. Instead they are used to wear down the surface by tearing the fibers and create sawdust-like waste rather than peelings. When applied lightly, scraping tools can produce a fine finish. As a rule, scraping tools are not honed after grinding. In fact, the burr formed during grinding is left on the edge and contributes to the tool's cutting action.

The most common scraping tools are square chisels, round nose chisels, parting tools and spear point chisels.

Square chisels are used with a scraping action. Although a standard woodworking chisel can be used for lathe work, it must be sharpened differently — a secondary bevel is not created on the cutting edge. For this reason it is usually best to have square chisels that are used only on a wood lathe as well as chisels that are used for general woodworking projects. Square chisels are used for smoothing, squaring a shoulder, forming short tapers and smoothing convex surfaces.

Round nose chisels are used with a scraping action and can be used in forming, large and small cove making, and hollowing.

The *parting tool* is most often used with a scraping action. It can be used for making narrow shoulders, cutting narrow Vs on tapers, cleaning work ends, sizing cuts and grooves, and cutting stock to length.

The *spear point chisel* is used for squaring during trim cuts, light chamfering, beads, cleans and forming or cutting Vs.

Sharpening Shearing Tools

Gouges are a little tricky to sharpen because they have a rounded rather than a flat cutting edge. In time you will probably develop your own method of sharpening a gouge, as there are really no hard-and-fast rules, except to keep a container of water close at hand and to dip the tool often and keep it cool. The most common method is to use a grinding wheel with a 60 to 80 grit aluminum-oxide wheel. A coarser wheel may be required for reconditioning nicked or damaged tips, but the finer grit is a good choice for

Square chisel.

Round nose chisel.

finish grinding of all lathe tools.

Although there are several styles of gouges — roughing and spindle or fingernail gouges, for example — they are all sharpened in the same manner. As a rule, hand grinding or honing a fresh bevel on a gouge takes too much time, so a bench grinder is the best way to reestablish this edge. Gouges are typically freehand ground, rotating through a smooth, continuous arc.

Begin by adjusting the tool rest so that its surface is horizontal and square to the face of the grinding wheel. Next, starting with the tool in an almost upside down position, lightly press the gouge into the face of the wheel at the proper bevel angle while at the same time rotating the tool. Maintain the proper bevel angle as you rotate the tool. One or two light passes should be all that is required to reestablish the proper bevel.

After grinding, it is necessary to hone gouges with a medium grit slip stone to remove the burr from the inside of the channel. This honing will help to make fine finish cuts. Next, lightly hone the beveled surface as well, but be careful not to create a secondary bevel.

A wood-turning skew is unique in that it has a double bevel and it is necessary to grind both when the tool becomes dull. As a rule, both bevels must be kept as flat as possible with not the slightest hint of a secondary bevel. Since it is usually only necessary to lightly grind a skew, this can be quickly accomplished on the side, rather than the face, of a grinding wheel. Do not, however, grind on the side of a wheel that is less than ¾″ wide.

Begin by adjusting the tool rest so that it is on a horizontal plane. Next, holding the skew level on the tool rest, lightly press one bevel into the side of the grinding wheel at the proper bevel angle. Never force the tool into the wheel, as this will cause too much metal to be ground off and build up excessive heat. After regrinding the first side of the skew, dip it in water to cool and repeat the process on the second bevel. A light touch is required.

A skew must be honed after grinding to remove the grinding burr. All that is usually required is to make a few passes over a medium grit bench stone. Hone just enough to remove the burr.

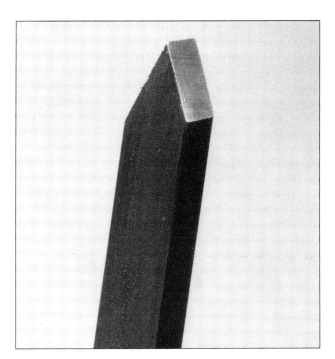

Parting tool.

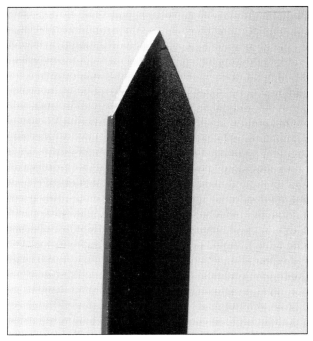

Spear point.

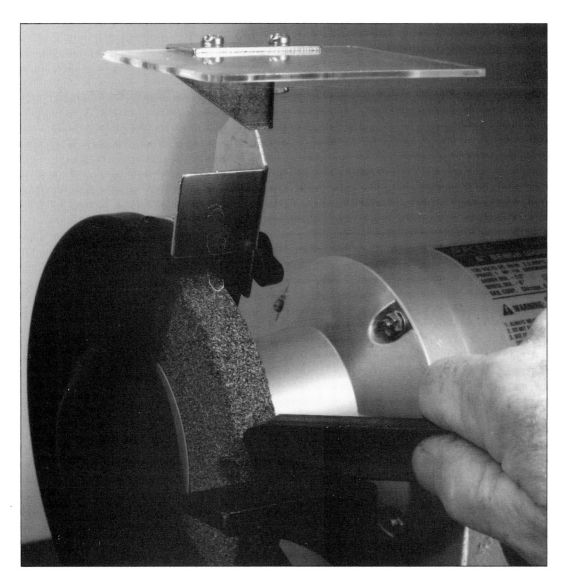

Twist a gouge when grinding to maintain the edge bevel.

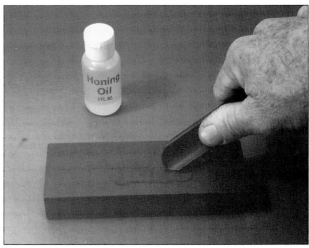

Hone a gouge after grinding.

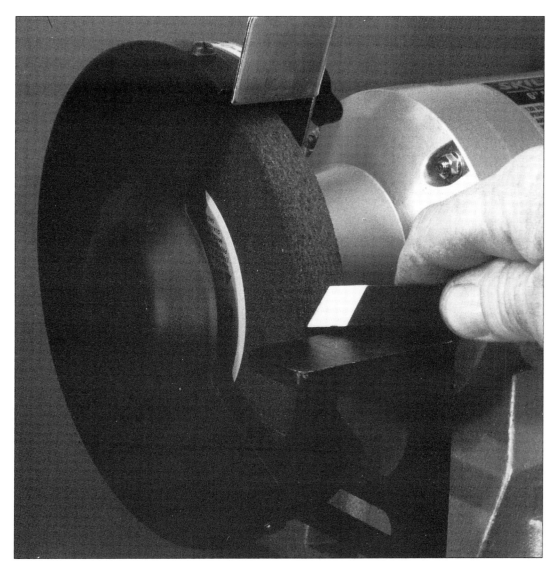

Grind a skew carefully to maintain the edge bevel.

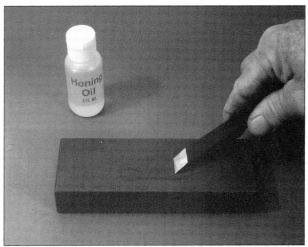

Hone a skew after grinding.

Sharpening Scraping Tools

Scraping tools for lathe work require frequent sharpening but never honing. In fact, the burr formed during grinding is left on the edge to help in the scraping action of the tool. Because they require frequent sharpening, scraping tools are best sharpened quickly. Just a light touch to the grinder is all that is required unless damage is present on the edge.

To sharpen a square chisel, begin by adjusting the tool rest of the grinder to a horizontal position. Next, holding the tool at the proper angle for the desired bevel (about 30°), lightly press it into the side of the grinder. Keep the tool level and do not force it into the wheel.

To sharpen a round nose chisel, begin by adjusting the tool rest of the grinder to a horizontal position. Next, holding the tool at the proper angle for the desired bevel (about 30°) and almost upside down, lightly press into the face of the wheel while at the same time rotating it to form a bevel on the

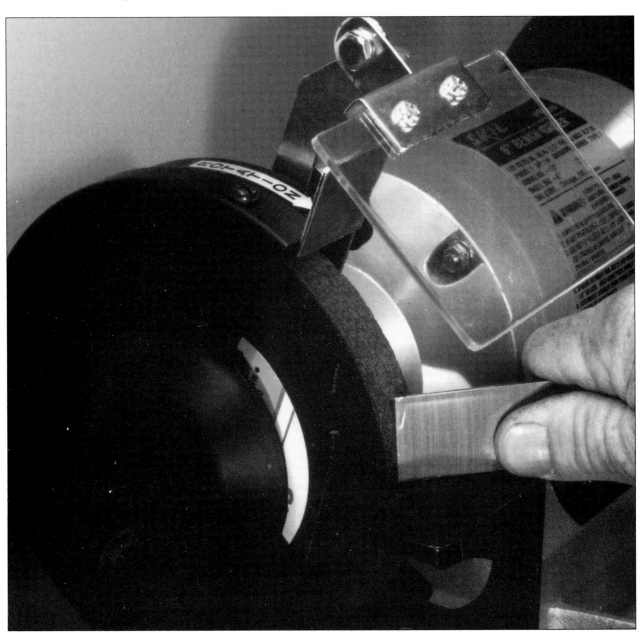

Grind a square chisel.

entire rounded edge. This should be done with a single sweeping motion.

A parting tool is relatively easy to sharpen providing you work carefully. Your intention is to keep the point of the parting tool centered on the shaft or the tool will be unbalanced. Some wood turners like to hone a parting tool after grinding; others think the additional work is worthless.

Spear point chisels are generally sharpened on the side of the grinding wheel unless damage to the edge is present. Simply freehand grind the bevels to restore the original angle of about 30°. Honing is not necessary or required for a spear point chisel.

Lathe tools should be protected when not in use to prevent damage. Store lathe tools in a special rack or drawer to protect the tips or cutting edges when not in use.

Grind a spear point chisel; honing is not necessary.

CHAPTER SEVEN

Sharpening Planer and Jointer Blades and Shaping Tools

The well-equipped woodworking shop will contain a number of power tools designed for shaping the surface of lumber. The more common of these are the *planer* or *jointer* and shapers such as a molding head cutter. Although other power tools, such as the router, can be used for shaping, we will limit our discussion in this chapter to these two basic types.

Bench-top planers are also available and are handy for jobsite work such as planing dimensional lumber. These units, often called *portable bench-top planers*, can be used for a variety of planing tasks where more than a hand-held unit is called for. They are indeed portable and relatively low priced (ranging from about $200 to $400).

All power planers (both stationary and handheld) operate on the same principle. A cylinder containing

Power Planers and Jointers

Generally speaking, two basic types of power planers or jointers are currently available — stationary and handheld or portable units. Stationary units are commonly found in larger woodworking shops and offer the advantage of being able to plane large, thick pieces of lumber. Combination jointer/planers are also popular because they can perform two tasks, jointing and planing. As a rule, power planers remain in the workshop rather than being transported.

Handheld planers are growing in popularity, at least in part because they are very portable. The typical unit is about the size of a conventional belt sander and can be used for a variety of planing tasks at the job site. Basically, hand planers can be used for all woodworking projects that would normally use a two-handed bench or block plane — door trimmings, edge planing, bevel planing and surface planing.

Portable, handheld planer.

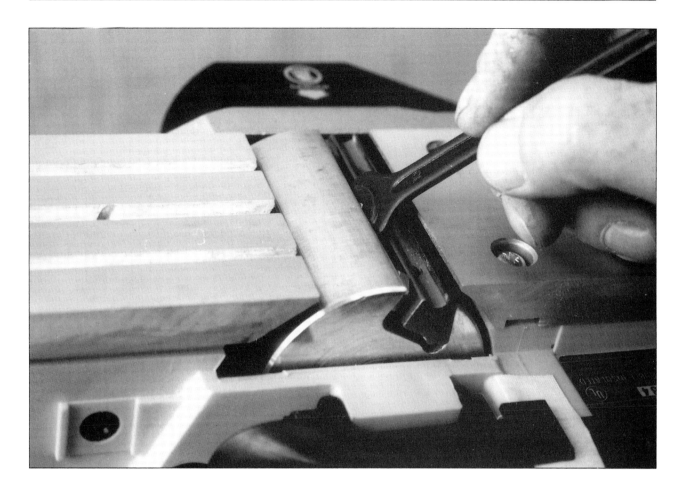

removable cutter blades spins below the surface of a two-part adjustable table. The depth of the planing action is controlled by adjusting the leading section of the table. Adjustments are typically in $1/128''$ (.2mm) increments with usual ranges from 0 to about $5/32''$ (4mm). The spinning rate is usually around 10,000 to 14,000 rpm, depending on motor size. Feed rate, of course, depends on the width of the material being planed.

Sharpening Planer and Jointer Blades

Planer blades can be removed from the cylinder before sharpening. Consult your owner's manual for directions on how to do this safely. Once the planer blade is in hand, look it over carefully. Most planer blades can be turned over to use the opposing edge before sharpening of both sides is required. If damage is present to the cutting edge this can be repaired if

Carefully remove the cutter blade from a portable planer.

not too severe. If nicks over about $1/32''$ are present, most experts agree that the planer blade should be replaced rather than repaired.

If damage to the power planer blade is slight, it can usually be ground to a point just below the nick, rebeveled and sharpened. Grinding planer blades requires some sort of jig or blade holder. Make such a holder by slot-cutting a piece of hardwood so the blade fits snugly while being ground.

To grind a power planer blade, begin by adjusting the tool rest on the grinder to form a 36° bevel and clamp a guide block to the shelf, parallel to the wheel face. Adjust this guide block so that the wheel will grind the blade lightly. A heavy grind, where much material is removed, will burn and ruin the blade. It is much better to make two or three light passes to

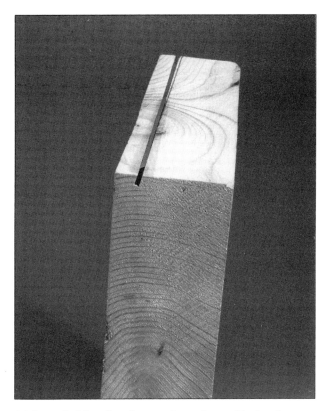

Make a holder for sharpening planer blades by cutting a block at the proper bevel angle.

restore the blade rather than to try to remove the damage in one pass. After the damaged area has been removed, sharpen as follows.

All planer blades have a flat side and an edge bevel side, not unlike conventional handheld bench or block planes. Unlike hand planes, which have a long blade, power planer blades are rather narrow and therefore do not lend themselves to being sharpened with any type of sharpening device other than those specifically designed for these blades. Power planer blades are commonly sharpened freehand on a bench stone.

Begin sharpening by laying the blade (flat side down) on a well-oiled, fine grit bench stone. Using a circular motion, work the flat side of the blade about twenty times. This action should result in a polish effect on the flat side of the blade. Next turn the blade over, hold it at the proper bevel angle (36°), bevel side down, and give it a few strokes to

restore the bevel. Check after about five strokes to make certain that the bevel is being honed evenly. Irregular polishing indicates that the blade is not being held level.

After about ten to fifteen strokes a wire edge will form on the bevel side of the power planer blade. Turn the blade over on the stone and make a few circular passes to remove this fine wire. Now a secondary bevel should be formed on the blade.

To create a secondary bevel, hold the blade flat on the stone, bevel side down, and raise it about 5° greater than the primary bevel. Make five passes over the stone and the secondary bevel should be formed. Check the edge of the cutter with a metal ruler or square to make certain that it is indeed square.

After sharpening, wipe the power planer blade with a clean, dry cloth and reinstall in the planer. Follow the manufacturer's directions so this is done

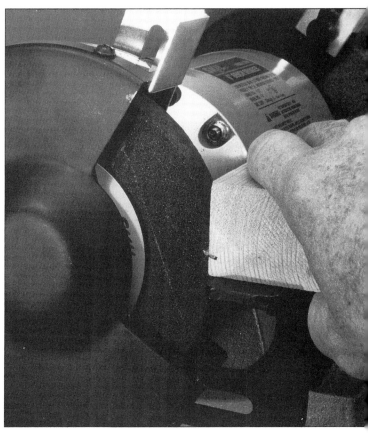

Grind a planer blade edge bevel with the aid of a custom slotted block.

properly. Misaligned planer cutter blades wear un-evenly and will not plane evenly.

It is also possible to touch up or whet power planer blades while they still in the machine. Keep in mind that this procedure is for touching up slightly dull planer blades, not full restoration type sharpening. First adjust the table so that both surfaces are on an even plane. Then position one cutter blade with its bevel parallel to the table surface. This can be done on stationary units by clamping the belt once the blade is in position. On handheld units, position the blade with the bevel parallel to the table

surface and simply hold it there with a screwdriver pressed into position between the drum and housing.

Wrap three-fourths of a flat bench stone in paper and place the wrapped part on the front table of the unit so that the stone just touches the blade bevel. The paper wrapping prevents scoring or scraping of the table face by the stone. Stroke the stone from one side of the cutter to the other several times and a wire edge will form. Count the number of strokes it takes you to accomplish this. Next lock the second cutter in the same position and repeat the procedure, giving the same number of strokes of the stone. Last,

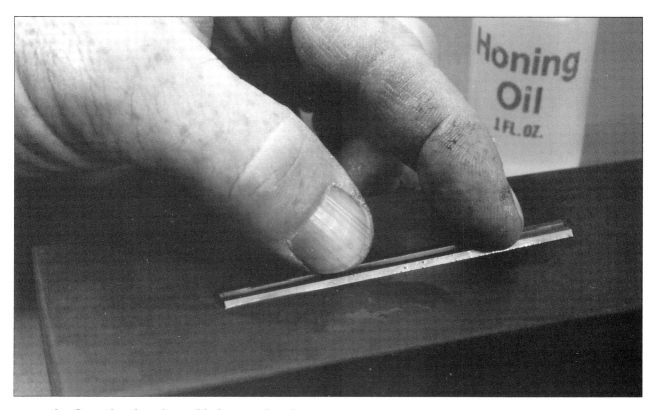

Hone the flat side of a planer blade on a bench stone; use lubricant.

remove the fine wire edge from both cutters using a small, fine grain stone held flat against the back of the cutters.

If desired for strength, you can also create a secondary bevel to the planer cutter blades. To do this, use a fine grit stone, wrapped in paper. Lay the stone flat, paper side on the table, and make five passes along the leading edge of the cutter blade. Revolve the drum and make the same number of passes over the second cutter.

Shapers

Shapers are commonly freestanding units that help you to make tongue-and-groove edges, shiplap edges, drop-leaf beads, moldings, and a variety of decorative designs in wood edges. Molding cutter blades are also available for table saws and radial arm saws, thus increasing the versatility of these common stationary

Use a screwdriver to hold the portable planer drum in place while working with a bench stone.

woodworking tools.

Shaper cutters resemble router bits in both use and configuration. They differ from router bits in that they are much larger and do not have a shaft. Instead they are mounted on a spindle. Shaper cutters cut from the side. Molding head cutters that are run in a table saw cut from below.

Sharpening Shaper Cutters

Shaper and molding head cutters are sharpened in very much the same way as large router bits. Essentially, only the flat side of the cutter is sharpened. As with router bits, it is important not to remove too much metal during the sharpening, as this will cause the cutter to be unbalanced during use.

Unless a cutter has been damaged, it usually can

be touched up rather quickly with a fine grit stone or file. Work carefully with the latter, as files are capable of removing excessive amounts of metal quickly.

Three-wing shaper cutters are commonly sharpened by whetting the flat faces adjacent to the edges. This is best accomplished with a suitable size, fine grit stone. A fine grit grinding wheel or vertical belt sander can also be used. Work carefully when using power equipment to sharpen, as it can change the contour of the face very quickly, most commonly making it convex rather than flat.

The tips of the cutters are not commonly sharpened in the home workshop as this could alter the

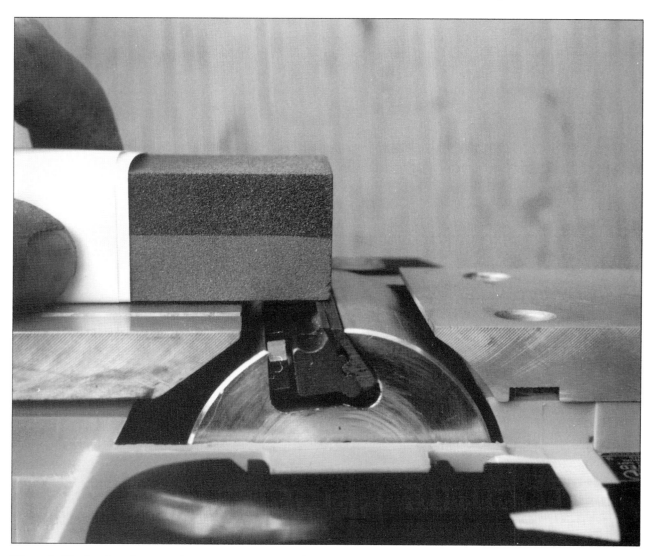

Wrap half of a bench stone in paper to protect the adjustable tabletop while sharpening.

balance of the cutter. Simply sharpen the flat face each time you touch up the cutter. After you have done this about five times, or if the cutter sustains damage, take the cutter to a professional sharpening service for reconditioning.

Once you have an understanding of the basic technique required for sharpening the faces of shaper cutters, you will see that it takes only a few minutes to touch up a typical cutter. Cutters perform much better after being touched up and your woodworking projects will benefit as well.

It is important to store your shaper cutters carefully so they will not be chipped or damaged. A storage rack for shaper cutters can be found in chapter twelve.

Sharpen the flat side only of a shaper cutter on a bench stone.

Shaper cutters can also be sharpened on a vertical sander.

CHAPTER EIGHT

Sharpening Router Bits

According to a recent survey in a popular do-it-yourself magazine, the most popular handheld electric tool in U.S. home workshops is the router. Little wonder, as this handy tool is almost indispensable for many different woodworking projects. Basically, a router consists of a high-speed electric motor capable of at least 25,000 rpm, a chuck for holding the router bit or cutter, and an adjustable base. There are one-handed routers for trimming plastic laminate, two-handed models for heavy-duty projects and two-handed plunge routers. In addition, most radial arm saws have a special router chuck on the side of the power unit that can be used to hold a router bit, thus adding versatility to the radial arm saw.

A router is very handy for many woodworking projects.

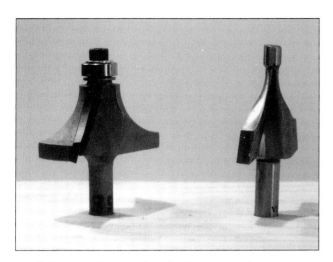

Carbide-tipped router bit (left) is much heavier than a conventional steel router bit.

Two basic materials are used in router bit construction: steel and carbide. As a rule, you can easily sharpen steel router bits with common sharpening tools, but must use diamond or ceramic tools for sharpening carbide-tipped router bits.

Because all router bits are used at extremely high speeds, balance of the bit is important for safety and performance. The do-it-yourself sharpener should be aware that it is possible to take the rotational balance out of a router bit by excessive grinding or sharpening. Therefore, do no more than touch up dull router bits, and do this not more than three times before taking the bit to a professional sharpening service for a full reconditioning. Although this suggestion is extreme, it does point out the need to be careful not to remove too much metal from router bits during the sharpening or touching up process. Unless damage is present, a dull steel router bit can be touched up quickly with a pocket stone or small handheld grinder. Carbide-tipped router bits, however, will require the use of a diamond abrasive.

Cleaning

In many cases, a router bit will not perform as expected because of a buildup of gum and pitch.

These deposits will cause a router bit to heat up excessively and move much slower through the work. It is best to keep your router bits clean and this can easily be done by first giving the bit a spray of silicone, then wiping clean. Burnt-on deposits of gum and pitch often require soaking in kerosene or other solvent to dissolve the buildup. After soaking, wipe the bit clean. Scrubbing with an old toothbrush may also be required.

After cleaning, and before use or storage, spray silicone lubricant on your router bits. This will help to make the bit cut smoother during use and make it easier to clean afterward. This coating will also protect the bit from rust during storage.

Sharpening Router Bits

As mentioned earlier, two materials are used in the construction of router bits, steel and carbide. Generally speaking, both steel and carbide-tipped router bits are sharpened in the same manner but, because carbide is harder than common tool steel, it must be sharpened with a diamond abrasive. Although carbide is indeed a hard material, it is no match for diamond abrasives and will be removed quickly, so work carefully.

Begin by cleaning the router bit to remove any resin or gum pitch. Next, carefully examine the bit in hand. If the bit has a ball bearing pilot wheel on the bottom, remove this before sharpening. In some cases a wrench must be used to remove the retaining nut, in other cases an Allen wrench. In any case, the pilot wheel must be removed prior to sharpening.

Sharpening Steel Router Bits
To touch up a steel router bit, use a fine grit abrasive stone, honing only the inside edge of the cutting edge or wing. When touching up a carbide-tipped router bit, use a diamond abrasive stone since regular abrasive stones will not cut carbide. Work this flat

surface toward the shaft of the bit rather than toward the outside edge or bevel. It is important to keep the stone flat on the surface so as not to distort or round over the face. Give about five strokes and look at the work. You should see evidence of honing right away. If two or more cutting edges are present on the bit, give five strokes to the other edges and examine them as well.

In most cases, touching up a router bit with a stone will require no more than about ten strokes per wing or cutting edge. If more material must be removed to restore the bit, grinding is usually called for and this should be done by a professional grinding service rather than by the do-it-yourself grinder.

Sharpening Carbide-Tipped Router Bits

Carbide-tipped router bits are sharpened in the same way as steel bits, using a diamond abrasive rather than a fine grit stone. Many people know that carbide is a hard material and tend to work more aggressively when sharpening. This is generally not necessary, as the diamond abrasive will cut carbide very quickly. As a rule, keep the cutting edge of the carbide-tipped router bit flat on the diamond abrasive. After no more than five strokes, stop and examine the work to see that the cutting surface remains flat. If more than one cutting face is being sharpened, sharpen all the same number of strokes. Stop when the surface is flat.

Although some router bits are piloted by a ball bearing wheel, many others have a pilot that is simply an extension of the bit and therefore cannot be removed. When sharpening this type of router bit, hone carefully and never allow the abrasive stone to touch the pilot.

Straight-flute router bits, of course, do not have any type of pilot and are therefore easier to touch up or sharpen. As with all other types of router bits, sharpen only the inside face of the cutter, never the bevel or outside edges. If more than one cutter is

Soak a well-used router bit before sharpening to remove pitch residue.

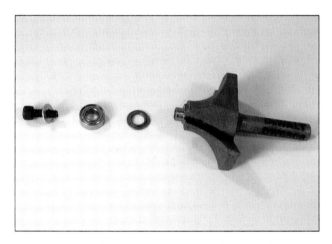

Piloted router bits consist of several parts that must be removed before sharpening.

present, sharpen all the same number of times—five strokes per face, for example.

Double-flute router bits (double cutters) have an almost flat angle just behind the cutting edge and a somewhat steeper angle just behind the first one. Using a stone, hone each of these surfaces, being careful not to cross over from one surface to the other. In some cases only a single bevel will be present and must be maintained during sharpening.

If the router bit is damaged—chipped, for example—grinding is usually called for and this should be done by a professional grinding service rather than the do-it-yourselfer. This applies to both steel and carbide-tipped router bits. It is important to remember that high-speed router bits must be balanced to cut properly. When extensive grinding is required to repair a damaged router bit, this should be done precisely, and this type of precision is generally beyond the capabilities of the average home woodworker.

Care of Router Bits

Router bits will last through many years of use if they are kept clean and sharp, are not forced through the work and are stored properly. More router bits are damaged during improper storage than by actual woodworking. To prolong their life store them in the original packaging or turn to chapter twelve for a router storage tray project that is worthwhile.

Hone only the flat sides of a router bit on a bench stone.

Protect router bits when not in use to prevent damage.

CHAPTER NINE
Sharpening Boring and Drilling Tools

Boring and drilling tools make holes in all types of materials, including wood, plastic, metal, glass and other modern materials. Since so many woodworking projects require boring of some kind, the average home workshop should be well equipped in this area. Handheld electric drills are one of the most popular tools in the United States and range from simple to downright amazing as far as capabilities. Battery-powered electric drills have become increasingly popular as well and offer portability with sufficient power for many boring tasks.

Because of the popularity of the handheld electric drill, a vast assortment of attachments can be used on almost any model. Currently available are attachments that can be used to quickly bore a hole in any material, pumps that can be used to transfer liquids (or pump out a basement), and even attachments for stirring paint. However, we will limit our discussion in this chapter to sharpening drill bits that are used for making holes.

It is probably safe to say that the most popular type of drill bit in use today is the common twist drill. These handy spiral shafts are simply chucked into the jaws of a drill and are used for making holes in almost any material. If materials other than wood are to be bored, special steel drill bits are commonly available to accomplish the task—tungsten bits for drilling steel, carbide-tipped bits for drilling concrete, and even special bits for drilling glass, for example.

Generally speaking, twist drill bits are not difficult to sharpen, and it should be mentioned that a number of special sharpening attachments and machines have come on the market in recent years to greatly simplify the process.

In addition to the ever popular twist drill bit, there are also a few other drill bits that are useful for special situations. Some worth mentioning include auger bits, spade bits, rim-cutting bits, Forstner bits, countersink bits and hole cutters. A brief discussion of each of these follows.

Auger bits were at one time used only in a hand-powered drill (commonly called a brace), but now there are auger bits designed for use in an electric

Twist drill bits are the most popular drill bits.

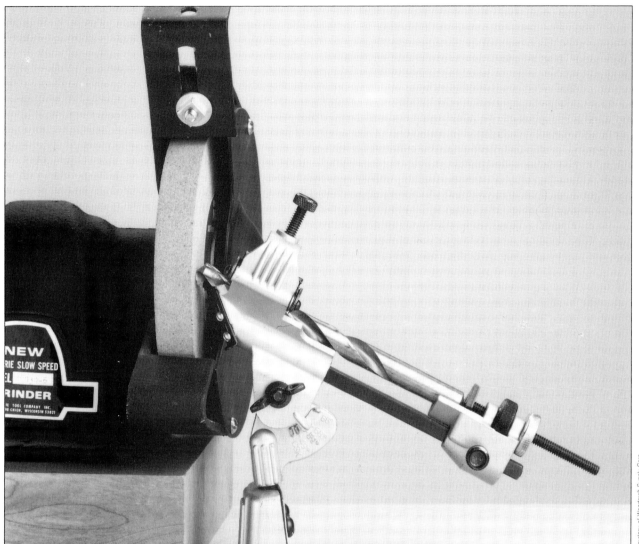

Courtesy of Woodcraft Supply Corp

This drill bit sharpening attachment for a bench grinder will help you to quickly sharpen twist drill bits.

drill. Older auger bits have a distinct, slightly pyramid-tipped shaft and are almost impossible to chuck into an electric drill; newer versions have a conventional shaft. Auger bits work best at low rpm's and should not be forced into the work. Use light pressure and allow the bit to bore a clean hole in the work.

Spade drill bits are simply a shaft of steel with a flattened end — the spade — that is beveled so that it scrapes more than actually bores as it passes through the work. Spade bits work fine as long as they are kept sharp; once they become dull they

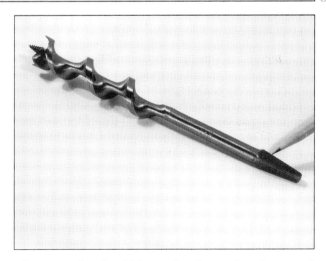

This auger bit should be used only in a hand-powered brace, never in an electric drill.

Spade bits are inexpensive and bore acceptable holes in wood.

require more force to use and, more often than not, will not bore correctly. Spade bits are inexpensive, handy for boring tasks that do not require precision, and easy to sharpen, as you will see in this chapter.

Rim-cutting drill bits make smooth, true holes and are relatively inexpensive. For this reason, rim-cutting bits are popular with fine woodworkers. The bit itself has a thin steel rim with an edge that cleanly bores through wood. Inside the rim of the bit is a sharp, chisel-like cutter that peels away wood after it has been rim cut. Rim-cutting drill bits work best when sharp and are not forced into the work. These drill bits have two cutting surfaces that must be sharpened by the do-it-yourselfer for optimum performance.

Forstner bits are similar to rim-cutting bits but offer the smoothest and cleanest of all holes. Forstner bits are also expensive when compared to other hole-making drill attachments, and thus are generally reserved for the finest woodworking projects.

Countersink drill bits perform two specialized functions for the woodworker: boring a pilot hole for a wood screw, and also boring a larger hole above the pilot hole so the screw head can be countersunk below the surface of the work. Countersink drill bits are handy as they perform two tasks at the same time. A variety of countersink drill bits are available, some resembling spade bits and others twist drills. All types can be sharpened in the home workshop.

The last drill bit that is handy to have around the home workshop is a special hole or circle cutter. Although there are several types, they all seem to have a twist drill bit center surrounded by a cutter for making the actual hole. The twist drill bit centers the unit while the outside cutter makes the hole. Some types have an adjustable arm for making the hole, while the more common types have a toothed

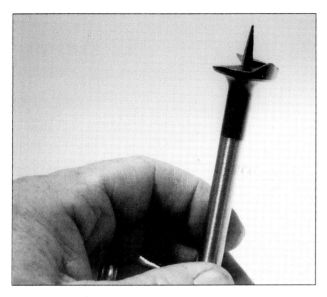

Rim-cutting bit.

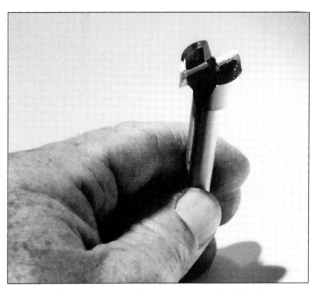

Forstner bits produce the cleanest of all holes in wood.

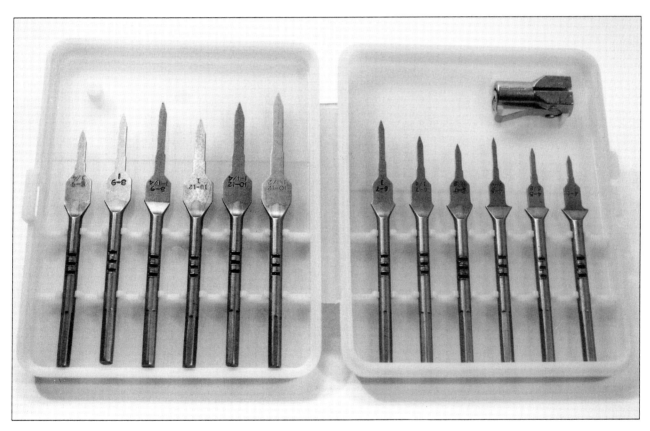

Countersink bits drill a pilot hole and a larger hole for concealing the head of a woodworking screw.

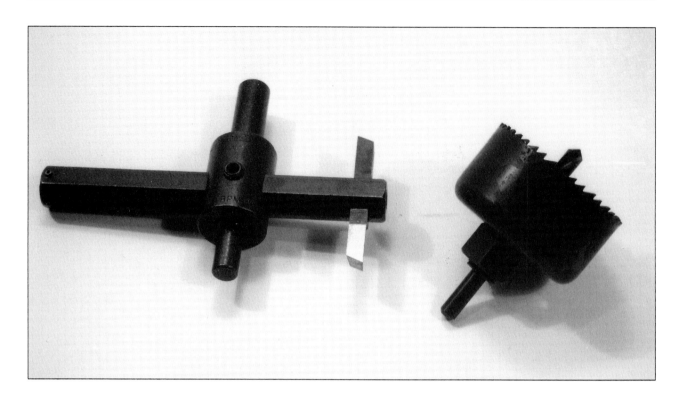

cylinder that makes the hole. Both types can be sharpened easily.

Circle cutter (left) and hole cutter can both be used in a drill.

Sharpening Twist Drill Bits

A twist drill bit has two cutting lips on the tip that are ground to the same length and at an angle of 59° to the axis of the bit. The drill must have lip clearance; that is, the metal must be ground off just back of the cutting lips to allow them to contact the work. Make yourself a template from cardboard (or, better yet, sheet steel) and use it to help you develop this angle.

A twist drill can be freehand sharpened by grinding either on the face or side of a bench grinder wheel. Begin by adjusting the grinder tool rest so that its surface is horizontal in relation to the wheel. Next, scribe a guideline on the tool rest to indicate a 59° angle. Now when the drill bit is laid parallel to this line, and flat on the tool rest, the tip of the drill bit will be in position for grinding at a perfect 59° angle.

Grind the drill bit by holding it securely at the 59° angle mark. Next, hold the cutting lip against the spinning grinding wheel and turn it slightly to the right and raise it slightly to obtain correct lip clearance. As you do this, keep in mind that you do not want to turn so much that you come in contact with the other lip. By turning the drill bit slightly, the surface back of the cutting lip is barely rounded. This is the compound angle you must achieve as it affords a stronger backing to the lips and will thus stay sharper longer.

As you grind, strive to keep the twist drill bit cool. This means working slowly so that it does not change color or get too hot to touch. In most cases, you will not require much grinding to sharpen a twist drill bit, so it should not get hot. If you are ever in doubt, dip the drill bit into water to keep it cool. Never allow it to get hot as this will destroy the temper of the steel and the bit will be useless.

Stop grinding often and check the angle of the

This bench grinder from Skil has a tool rest with a slot designed for sharpening twist drill bits.

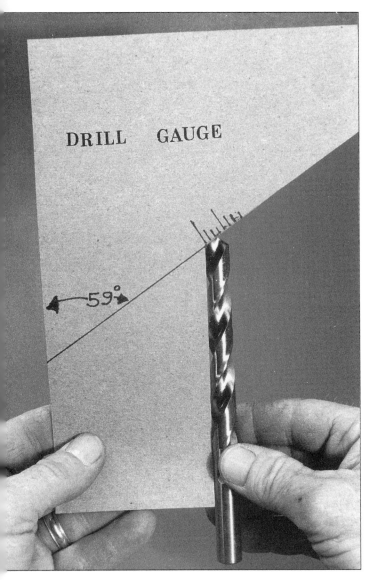

Make a template from cardboard or sheet metal for checking the grind on twist drill bits.

twist drill bit on your template guide. Once you are satisfied with the bevel, test the drill bit by drilling a hole. Simply chuck the newly sharpened drill bit into a drill and make a hole in a piece of scrap lumber. When sharpened properly a twist drill should practically pull itself into the work with little pressure required on your part.

A real test of sharpness for a twist drill bit is to drill a piece of steel or soft metal. When a twist drill bit has been sharpened properly, each lip will cut a spiral coil of metal as it bores a hole into metal. Use

a low rpm speed and do not force the drill into the work.

Sharpening Spade Drill Bits

Spade drill bits can be sharpened by two basic methods, filing and grinding. A file is handy for quick touch-ups, but a bench grinder should be used if the spade bit has been damaged.

To file a spade bit, first fasten it between the jaws of a bench vise with the cutting edges of the bit at a comfortable distance above the jaws. Most spade bits have two cutting edges, one on either side of the pointed tip, while others may have only one cutting edge. In any case, the file is pushed into and over the cutting edge. If required, as with some of the larger spade bits, lift the back of the file gradually through each stroke to produce a slightly crowned surface on the topside of the cutting edge. A few strokes of the file should be all that is required, unless there is a nick in the cutting edge. If this is the case, you must work longer with the file to remove the damaged area to restore the bit's cutting edge.

If you are removing a damaged area on a spade bit with a file, remove only enough of the cutting edge to eliminate the damage. If the spade bit has two cutting surfaces, and only one side is damaged, you must remove equal amounts of steel from both sides of the bit or it will be unbalanced and will not bore correctly.

If the spade bit has two cutting edges, sharpen one with the file before working on the other side. Strive to maintain the original bevel and angle of the cutter. By filing into the cutting edge of the spade bit, you virtually eliminate the possibility of a wire edge forming on the cutting edge. One other good reason for filing a spade bit (as opposed to grinding) is that the bit never gets too hot from the sharpening, and the original temper of the steel will remain intact.

After the cutting edges of the spade bit have been sharpened with a file, turn your attention to the pointed tip of the bit. Unless the tip has been damaged, only a few strokes of the file should be required to touch up the tip. Damaged areas must, of course, be removed with the file. When filing the tip, you should maintain the slight bevel to the edge (approximately 5°).

Last, turn your attention to the sides of the spade bit. These should be filed so they are square — that is, with no bevel. If the sides have nicks or chips do not remove too much steel. Simply square off the edges.

Many woodworkers prefer to sharpen spade bits on a bench grinder or vertical sander and this is certainly a fast and efficient way of accomplishing the task. Success, in this case, depends on adjusting the tool rest at an angle that will produce an 8° bevel on the cutting edge of the bit. It is also important to keep the shaft of the spade bit resting firmly on this base, while at the same time keeping the cutting surface, which is being ground, perpendicular to the spinning stone.

Grind with a light touch when sharpening a spade bit on a bench grinder. Do not attempt to remove too much of the metal, only enough to put a keen edge on the cutters. This assumes, of course, that no damage has been done to the cutting edge, in which case the cutting surface must be ground to below the damaged area.

Keep in mind, when grinding a damaged area on a spade bit, that both sides of the bit must be equal.

A file can be used for sharpening spade drill bits.

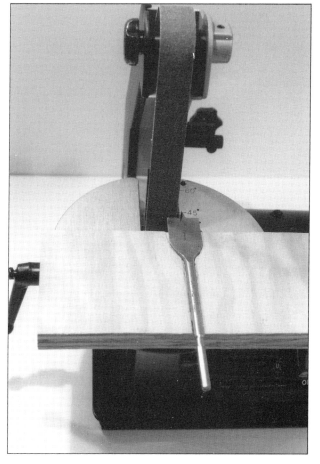

A verticle belt sander, with an adjustable table, can be used for sharpening spade drill bits.

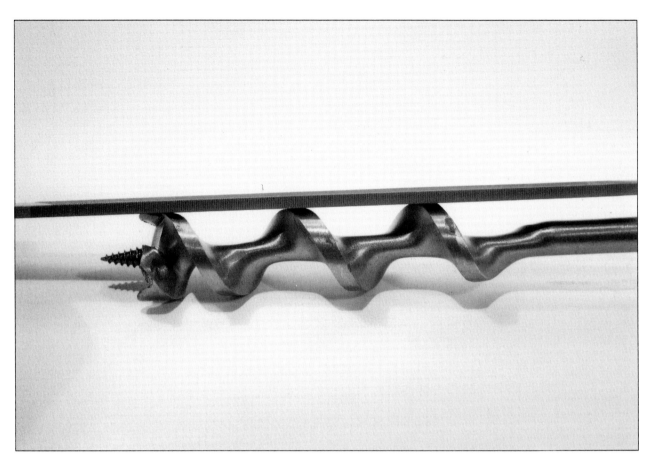

For example, if you remove ¹⁄₆₄″ on one side of the bit to eliminate a nick, the other side of the bit must also have an equal amount of steel removed. Failure to do this will cause undue stress on the longer side of the bit, and it will not bore well.

As with all sharpening on a grinding wheel, it is important that the bit not be allowed to heat up excessively. When this happens the metal will turn blue and the temper will surely be lost. Grind lightly and allow the bit to cool naturally if you suspect that it is becoming hot.

After the cutting edges of the spade bit have been ground to an 8° bevel, turn your attention to the tip and sides of the bit. Remove any damage and grind the tip to about 5°. Grind the sides of the spade bit square.

Use a flat file to remove any burrs on the spirals of an auger bit.

Sharpening Auger Bits

Auger bits were at one time designed only for use in a hand-powered brace but now there are auger bits for electric drills. Never, however, use an auger bit that was made for a brace in an electric drill. Both types are sharpened in the same manner. When an auger bit is sharp, it is very easy to use and will help you to bore a clean hole, the size of which is determined by the diameter of the bit itself. An auger bit should last a lifetime with just a minimum of care in the form of keeping it lightly oiled to prevent rust and touching up the cutting edge as often as required.

As a rule, the best way to sharpen an auger bit is with a file and finish off with a whetstone. Use a small triangular file for small auger bits and a larger flat file for larger bits. Use a fine grit whetstone of suitable size for the final sharpening.

To file an auger bit, begin by placing it on a bench horizontally and lightly file off the parts of the spiral and rim cutters that may have been bent outward during use. This is done by holding the file as shown on page 86. Care must be exercised here to keep the edges their approximate diameter all around. Keep the file laying flat and it will remove only bent or curled metal as necessary.

The next step is to file the two cutters on the face of the bit. This is done by holding the bit as shown in the photo below, and filing only the inside of the spur at the front of the cutting edge. The filing angle is important and you should strive to duplicate the original edge with the file. Work care-

fully so you do not file the spurs or rim cutters. After both cutters have been filed, finish off the sharpening with a whetstone for a keen edge.

Last, turn your attention to the screwlike point of the auger bit. Touch up as required to form a point, being careful not to file the threads of the point. After all sharpening, give the auger bit a light coating of silicone spray or lightweight oil.

Sharpening Rim-Cutting Bits

The rim-cutting bits in popular use today will enable you to make a clean, crisp hole in almost any type of lumber, assuming of course that the bit being used is sharp. Actually, a rim-cutting bit is sharpened in a manner similar to that used for sharpening an

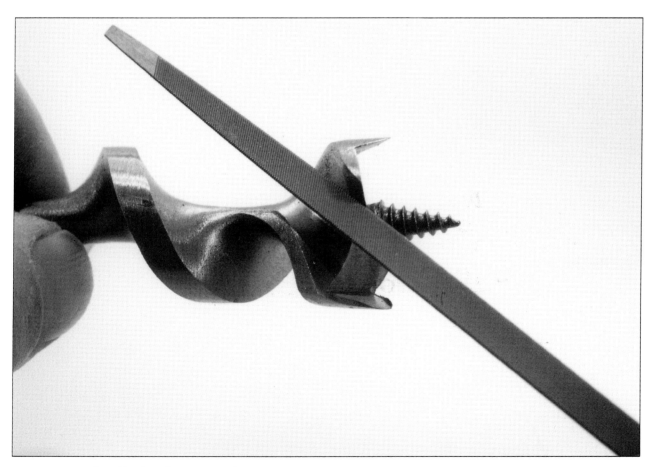

Use a triangular file for sharpening the cutters on an auger bit.

Hone the outside of a rim-cutting bit with a small pocket stone.

auger bit. The main difference is that the rim-cutting bit is easier to sharpen, for it has only one cutting edge and a spur (the part of this bit that scribes the hole being bored).

I have found that the easiest way to sharpen a rim-cutting bit is with a slim taper three-sided file. Do this with the bit securely fastened in a bench vise at a height that is comfortable for filing. Begin by noting if any damage has been done to the cutting face of the bit. If this is the case, you must file the cutting edge past this point. If no damage has been done, simply file the cutting edge to a 25° bevel on one side of the cutter. Next turn your attention to the other side of the cutting edge. This side is flat and should be touched up with the file as well.

After the cutting edge has been filed suitably, turn your attention next to the spur or rim of the bit. This part of the bit is important from the standpoint of having a clean hole, so it must be given a sharp edge. The rim cutter can be touched up with either a file or small stone. Work carefully to sharpen

this edge and remove any burrs that may have formed during use. Generally speaking, a few passes of a file or stone should be all that is required to sharpen an undamaged spur. If damage is present, it must be removed and a new cutting edge established.

The last step in sharpening a rim cutting bit is to touch up the point of the bit. In most cases this is a three-sided point and should be filed so that all three sides are flat and crisp. Once again, a slim taper file is a good tool choice for this task.

Sharpening Forstner Bits

Forstner bits are similar to rim-cutting bits in that they produce a clean hole with sharp edges. They differ in that Forstner bits have two half-moon rims that guide the bit in use. There are also two cutters inside the bit to remove wood quickly and cleanly. As a rule, Forstner bits work best when run at slow speeds—below 250 rpm—and when not forced into the work.

Unless they are damaged, Forstner bits do not require extensive sharpening. Simply touch up the outside edge of the rim with a file to remove any metal burrs. Next touch up the inside of the rim with a small, fine grit slip stone. Last, touch up the cutters inside the bit are with a small slip stone as well. Simply clean up the edge of the bevels on these cutters.

Sharpening Countersink Bits

Countersink drill bits seem to wear most at the point of the bit and this is where you should turn your sharpening attention. As a rule, unless it has been

Sharpen countersink drill bits (at right) by using a circular motion on a bench stone.

Sharpen the outside of Forstner bit on a bench stone.

damaged, a countersink drill bit can be sharpened on a small whetstone. After the cutting edges have been whetted, lay the bit on a flat surface and pass the stone over it several times while at the same time applying finger pressure so that the stone can cut true. When working, keep in mind that the point must remain along the center axis of the countersink bit, or it will not drill holes that are true. Work carefully, and in a few minutes you can restore a countersink drill bit to like-new sharpness.

Sharpening Hole Cutters

The most common type of hole-cutting attachment for drills in use today consists of a twist drill bit, a mandrel, and a cylinder-shaped hole cutter. As a rule, the drill/mandrel part of this cutter can be used with a wide range of cylinder cutters. The cutters themselves are sized from ½" to 6" in diameter. Although several different types of hole cutters are available, they all work in a similar manner.

In use, a hole-cutter cylinder is selected for the task at hand and is fastened—either by a threaded connection, Allen set screw or overfitting collar—to the twist drill/mandrel. The twist drill keeps the unit centered while the cylinder cutter bores a hole in the material. There are several different types on the market designed for most types of materials including wood, plaster, plastic, steel and concrete. Hole-cutting attachments for drills offer a quick way to bore a hole but do not make as clean a hole as a rim-cutting or Forstner bit.

Sharpening a hole cutter involves two tasks—sharpening the twist drill and sharpening the cutter cylinder. Since sharpening twist drill bits was covered

Hole saw must be disassembled before sharpening.

Use a small triangular file for sharpening the teeth on a hole saw.

earlier in this chapter, that information will not be duplicated here. Instead we will turn our attention to sharpening the cutter cylinder.

Begin by disassembling the twist drill/mandrel from the hole-cutting cylinder. Remove the twist drill from the mandrel (commonly fastened in place with an Allen head or slotted head screw). Sharpen the twist drill bit as described earlier in this chapter or replace it with a new twist drill bit. Next examine the teeth of the cutter. You will notice that every other tooth is bent outward, similar to a conventional saw blade. After sharpening, each of these teeth must be bent in or out alternately. This task is best accomplished with a special saw-setting tool—a plier-like tool placed over each tooth and squeezed to form a perfect set or bend.

Sharpening a hole-cutting cylinder begins very much the same as saw sharpening. First, use a flat file to make all of the teeth the same height, slightly flattening the tops to get all of the teeth in line. Next, file all of the gullets and tooth faces. Some hole cutters have round gullets, which indicates that a slim round file must be used for the sharpening. Other brands of hole cutters have V-shaped gullets, requiring the use of a slim three-sided file for the sharpening.

Filing the gullets and teeth of a hole cutter goes easier if the cylinder is clamped into a bench vise. File a few teeth, then loosen the vise, rotate the cylinder and retighten the vise jaws. Work carefully to duplicate the bevel angle of each tooth. After filing all teeth, set the teeth alternately in and out, using a saw tooth setting tool. Reassemble the parts and make a test hole with the cutter.

CHAPTER TEN
Sharpening Saw Blades

Since saw blades probably represent the largest group of tools in the woodworking shop, it is to your advantage to know what constitutes a sharp saw. A sharp saw blade helps you to make straight, clean cuts in any material while a dull or nicked saw blade results in ragged or burned cuts.

Generally speaking, we find two basic types of saw blades, circular and straight. By far the largest group are circular saws, including handheld circular saws, table and radial arm saws. Straight blade saws

Circular saws are easily the most popular of all electric saw types.

include handsaws, saber or reciprocating saws and band saws. As a rule, hacksaw blades are simply discarded when dull, rather than being sharpened.

Circular Saw Blades

Since the procedures for sharpening circular saw blades — as used in handheld circular, table and radial arm saws — are the same, we will discuss these types of blades as if all circular saw blades were interchangeable.

Before we can begin discussing how to sharpen circular saw blades, we first need to take a look at the different types. Although all circular saw blades are sharpened in a similar manner, some filing tasks are necessary on some blades and not on others. Let's take a brief look at the more popular types of circular saw blades before we get into the mechanics of sharpening.

Combination circular saw blades are so named because they will crosscut, miter and rip. Most manufacturers offer four types of combination circular saw blades: *all-purpose* (which is flat ground) for smooth cutting in any direction through all types of wood; the *chisel tooth* (also flat ground) for fast, rugged general types of cuts; *planer* (flat ground) with fast-cutting teeth that are set for wider clearance; and the *planer II* (hollow ground) for fast and exceptionally smooth cutting. This last saw blade is ideal for furniture and cabinet work with teeth that are hollow ground for clearance.

Rip circular saw blades, as the name implies, are used for making rip cuts in both hard and soft woods. They are commonly filed square to cut wood with the grain, and as a result are not recommended for crosscutting lumber. The teeth on a rip circular saw blade are shaped like tiny chisels and cut chips in a similar manner. One popular variation of the standard rip circular saw blade called the *framing/rip* is used for cutting dimensional lumber — 2 × 4 and 2 × 6

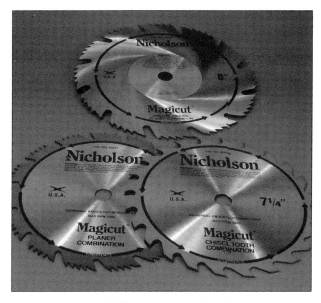

There are several different types of combination circular saw blades.

lumber — during construction of wood frame buildings. These blades, although not true rip in design, produce acceptable cuts in lumber and, of possible greater importance, do the cutting very quickly.

Plywood circular saw blades are suitable only for cutting plywood, hence the name. Plywood blades are available in both flat ground and hollow ground versions. The flat ground blade allows for smooth

Rip circular saw blade.

cutting of plywood paneling, plywood and laminates, and can be used when an occasional nail will be encountered (such as when cutting plywood subfloors that have been nailed in place). The hollow ground plywood circular saw blade is generally considered the top-of-the-line blade for cutting plywood. It has beveled teeth and allows virtually splinter-free cutting. The hollow ground plywood blade is used extensively in the building of plywood furniture largely due to the smooth cuts that it produces.

Carbide-tipped circular saw blades offer a cutting performance that lasts up to fifteen times as long as conventional steel-toothed circular saw blades. Although a number of different types of carbide-tipped circular saw blades are used for different cutting applications, a good rule to follow is: The more carbide teeth on a blade, the smoother the finished cut will be. Currently available are 8- and 10-toothed carbide blades, which are suitable for rough, framing types of cuts. Carbide-tipped blades with more teeth — up to sixty teeth per blade — are more suitable for finished cuts on all type of wood. As an example, a cabinet shop will probably have a 60-toothed carbide blade for making finish cuts. The long cutting life of carbide-tipped blades can be directly attributed to the pieces of carbide that are welded to the cutting

edges of a circular saw blade. Carbide is so hard that it cannot be sharpened in a conventional manner — with a file — as all other types of circular saw blades can be. Sharpening carbide teeth on a circular saw blade requires a special diamond file or diamond chip abrasive sharpening device. Since these special sharpening tools are not likely to be in the average woodworking shop, we will not discuss how to sharpen carbide-tipped circular saw blades in this book. It is advisable to have carbide-tipped circular saw blades professionally sharpened. This service is not very expensive and can be done only with special tools.

To be sure, there are other types of circular saw blades. Some can be sharpened (such as dado blades), while others do not lend themselves to being touched up — abrasive masonry and tile-cutting blades for instance. Generally speaking, if the blade has teeth that can be ground with a standard file, then it is safe to say it can be sharpened by home workshop methods. Read on through this chapter and you will learn the general procedures that may be required and apply them as necessary for your circular saw blade sharpening task at hand.

A sharp saw blade cuts efficiently and smoothly. When you find yourself pushing harder to make a

Carbide-tipped circular saw blades stay sharper much longer than conventional steel blades.

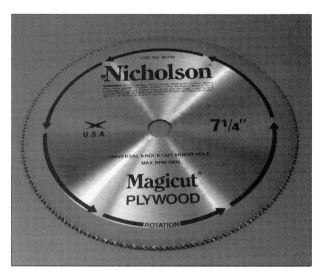

Plywood circular saw blade.

cut, or if the finished cut is ragged or blackened, chances are very good that the blade needs to be sharpened. In extreme cases, the saw blade may actually produce a cloud of smoke as it burns through the work rather than cutting. Carefully inspect your circular saw blade before each use. If you discover wood gum residue around the teeth, or if the tips of the teeth appear black, the blade will require some service to get it back into shape.

Sharpening a Circular Saw Blade

There are four separate steps to the sharpening process for flat ground circular saw blades. These are (in order of procedure): jointing, gumming, setting and filing. Hollow ground circular saw blades are sharpened in three distinct operations: rounding, gumming and filing. You should know from the outset that some aids will make these sharpening operations easier to accomplish and it may therefore be helpful to mention them in passing.

Jointing is an operation where all of the teeth of a saw blade are ground to the same height. This operation is most easy to accomplish on a standard table saw or radial arm saw. For handheld circular saws, one must accomplish this operation by adjusting the saw table so that the tips of the blade just pass below the table and touch the stone. Once you have a clear understanding of how to joint a circular saw blade, you will be able to make adjustments to a handheld saw with a sense of purpose. Just remember to disconnect the unit from the power source before beginning.

Since a table saw is the easiest aid for jointing, we will carry on this discussion using one in the demonstration. Begin by first unplugging the table saw for safety's sake. Next, run the blade up (or the table down, as the case may be) so that several inches of the blade are exposed. Then check the squareness of the blade with a framing square. Strive for a perfect

Adjust the table saw blade to 90° with a try square.

90° angle between the blade and tabletop by making suitable adjustments.

Adjust the height of the saw blade so that it now extends above the tabletop only a fraction of an inch ($\frac{1}{1000}''$). Lay a scrap piece of lumber on the table and adjust the blade so that all teeth lightly touch the underside. Now use a large Carborundum stone in place of the scrap lumber and spin the blade in the normal operating direction — forward. The object here is to make all the teeth the same height without grinding off too much. Of course, if even one tooth has been damaged, then all the teeth on the blade must be ground down to equal this height. This just might be the time you consider buying a new blade

Jointing a table saw blade.

Some sharpening aids take the work out of sharpening circular saw blades.

or having the damaged blade ground by a professional. In most cases, however, jointing of a normally dull saw blade is a simple process.

Some authorities recommend jointing the saw with the electric motor running. Although I do not recommend this for your first attempt at jointing, I think it is a worthwhile approach once you have a fair understanding of the procedure involved. Jointing is often done with the blade reversed in the saw and spun backward, and this method reduces the potential for damage to either the stone or blade. One last tip worth mentioning is that applying a coating of carbon (formed by holding the blade over a burning candle flame) to the tip of each tooth prior to jointing enables you to see when each tooth has been touched by the stone. Lighting from the side also helps to see when the carbon has been scraped off each tooth.

After you are satisfied that the circular saw blade has been sufficiently jointed, readjust the blade so that the gullets are in a position to be filed.

Gumming is the second sharpening operation for circular saw blades and can be done with a round file. A 7/32″ round chain saw file works well for this operation. If you have the specialized equipment (handheld electric grinder), this operation is easier to accomplish, but it can be done with care and a good round file. Begin by adjusting the saw table so that the gullet of each tooth just clears the tabletop. Then, with a soft black pencil held in position — just touching a point below each gullet — spin the blade and draw a perfect circle around the entire blade. After the circle is complete, remove the pencil and raise the blade up to a comfortable filing position. Now, slowly turn the blade once again and note where

Use a pencil to draw a line just below the gullets on the blade. Spin the blade by hand for this.

each gullet is in relationship to the pencil line. All gullets should be an equal distance from the circle. The next step involves filing each gullet so that they are all as deep as the pencil line circle. In short, each gullet will have an equal depth.

The gumming operation restores the teeth to their correct height when they have been worn shallow by repeated sharpening. It is therefore not necessary to gum a saw blade every time it is sharpened. As a rule of thumb, a circular saw blade should be gummed after every third or fourth sharpening.

When gumming a circular saw blade with a chain saw file, it is important that you do not work any gullet too long. To do so would cause a gullet to heat up beyond temper, resulting in bluing and, in time, a fracture in the area. This is especially true when grinding gullets with a handheld electric grinder. Working with a round chain saw file reduces the chances of damage.

When filing gullets, push the file through the slot, turning it slightly on each pass. Simply deepen the gullet to the pencil line while at the same time keeping the gullet the same in other respects. Do not, for example, file the sides of the gullet. Instead file the bottom of the gullet itself. You may find it helpful to file only halfway down on each gullet on the first pass around the blade. Then, on the second pass deepen the gullet to the pencil line. After all of the gullets have been so deepened, remove the saw blade from the table saw (or from the handheld circular saw, if that is what you are working on) for the third operation in the sharpening process.

Setting the teeth on a circular saw is the next step in the sharpening process. Setting the saw means bending the teeth alternately right and left to provide clearance. If the teeth are not accurately set, more strain is placed on some teeth than others, which can cause them to crack or (in extreme cases) break off. Unevenly set teeth may also cause the saw to chatter as it cuts through work and will most

A power grinder can also be used for grinding the gullets. Work carefully so you don't remove too much metal.

Use a chain saw file to file the gullets to the pencil line around the entire blade.

commonly result in a ragged and rough cut.

A circular saw blade that has little set will bind or jam in the cut simply because there is not enough room for the waste wood to be thrown out of the cut. If the teeth are set more on one side than on the other, the saw will wander to the side of the heaviest set and breakage of the teeth will soon occur. As you can see, proper set is important for efficient circular saw operation, so it must be done with care.

Generally speaking, there are two approaches to the setting operation for a circular saw blade, (1) using the stake-and-anvil method and (2) using a special saw setting tool. Many do-it-yourselfers like the stake-and-anvil method, but bear in mind that this rather specialized tool must either be made or purchased. See the illustration below for setup of the anvil.

If the stake-and-anvil method is used, the saw blade should be placed on the stake and the beveled anvil adjusted to give the required set. Then set the teeth using a hammer and metal punch. Work carefully to ensure that the set of each individual tooth does not extend more than one-quarter of the depth down the tooth.

Circular saw teeth can also be set with the use

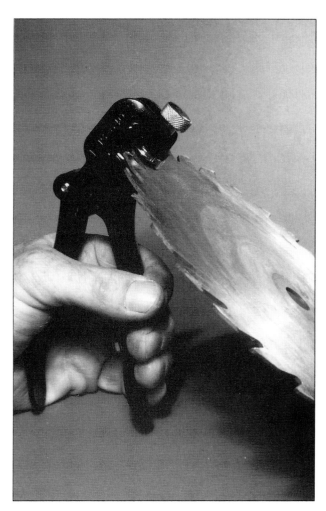

A saw set is useful for evenly setting all circular saw teeth.

of a special tool designed for the purpose. Special combination tools for sawtooth setting look like a specialized pair of pliers and come with a gauge attachment to regulate the set of each tooth. In addition, special graduated slots give the desired depth to the tooth set. When placing this tool on the saw, it should be allowed to drop until the point of the saw tooth touches the bottom of the slot. The tooth can then be bent until the gauge touches the side of the blade.

Filing is the last operation in the sharpening process for circular saw blades and is done with the saw blade sandwiched between two wooden blocks and held tightly in a bench vise. You can easily make a pair of filing blocks from ¾″ plywood. Simply cut

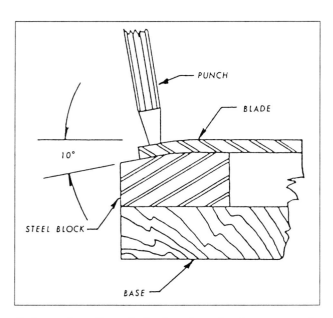

Stake-and-anvil method of setting circular saw teeth.

two circles 1″ less in diameter than your saw blade — two 9″ plywood disks for a 10″ circular saw blade, for example. If you have a variety of sizes of saw blades — 6″, 7½″, 8″ and 10″ — make up pairs of plywood disks for each size blade. They will last a lifetime and greatly simplify blade filing in the future.

Since the bevels on the cutting teeth vary with each type (a ripsaw blade being different from a combination blade, for example), this is the operation where you must take special care. As general guidelines, a slim taper file is good for sharpening combination blade teeth, while a flat file is used on the rakers. Although different saw blades require different filing angles, the basic techniques are the same. Let's now take a look at how to sharpen a few different types of circular saw blade designs.

To file a ripsaw blade, use a 6″ regular taper file with two round edges and file straight across the outside edge of the teeth in the direction of the saw set. This, of course, means filing alternate teeth, then turning the saw in the vise before filing the remainder. A swivel-head vise saves lots of time when filing, as

Make a plywood disk to hold circular saw blades during sharpening.

File Selection Chart for Saw Tooth Sharpening

Crosscut 5 point and 5½ point	6″ regular taper file
Crosscut 6, 7, 8 and 9 point	4½″ regular taper file
Crosscut 10, 11 and 12 point	5½″ slim taper file
Rip 4½, 5, 5½ and 6 point	4½″ regular taper file
Coarse rip 4 point	6″ regular taper file

the blade does not have to be removed to file alternate teeth; simply swivel the vise instead. Extreme care must be taken to maintain the original hook, shape and angle of each tooth. If you are in doubt as to the proper angle of the bevel, you can check a new, unused blade (if one is around the shop) or possibly consult the blade manufacturer. When you purchase a new blade, you might want to check the angle of the bevel with a protractor and note this angle in a notebook used for important information around the shop. Finish off sharpening by checking the hook of each tooth and rounding the gullets.

Filing cutoff saw blades — a plywood blade, for example — requires a similar approach except that a thin taper file is used for the process. Select a taper file to suit the size of the teeth and take care to maintain the original bevel and angle of each tooth. The teeth should be of uniform width and shape and the gullets of equal depth and width as well. (Note that the gullets on this type of saw blade tend to be shallow in depth.) In addition, every tooth should have the same amount of bevel, which is most commonly about 12° to 15°, being shorter for softwood and longer for hardwood.

File both faces of each tooth to bring it to a point, but don't continue any further as this will shorten the teeth. Finish sharpening by rounding out the gullets with a suitable sized round and narrow file.

When sharpening a planer circular saw blade, still another technique is used for the process. First file the raker teeth with the aid of a raker gauge, which ensures that the rakers are kept at the recommended depth below the cutting teeth. As a rule, raker teeth are commonly 1/64" below the cutting teeth.

If you have a set of dado blades—or dado head, as this setup is often called—you will know when they need sharpening, as the quality of the dado will not be uniform. Since sharpening a dado head requires more specialized equipment than the average home workshop usually contains, have your dado head sharpened by a professional saw sharpening service. It is important to bear in mind that a blunt dado head can be a hazard to work with because of the nature of the cutting this blade is expected to perform.

Some dado sets are composed of a combination of saw blades and spacers, or some type of adjusting mechanism that "wobbles" the blade or adjusts the width of the cut. As a rule, if the individual blade or blades can be disassembled into single blade components, each can be sharpened in the home workshop using methods described earlier in this chapter.

Sharpening a circular saw blade is not difficult but does require your fullest attention during all four sharpening operations. Work carefully and you should be able to restore a circular saw blade with just a bit of effort. Keep in mind that the average charge for sharpening a standard steel blade—that is, other than a carbide-tipped or dado head cutter—is around five to fifteen dollars. It is therefore possible to realize a significant savings many times a year simply by doing all but the most difficult sharpening yourself.

After you have sharpened a circular saw blade, chances are very good that you will want to press it into service as soon as possible. Once the blade has been reinstalled in the saw, it is wise to give the blade a light coating of silicone spray. This will not only help to prevent surface rust but will also lubricate it during the cutting process and thus keep it running cooler. This translates into a longer life for

File the teeth in a circular saw blade carefully.

Steel dado blade sets can be sharpened easily in the home workshop.

the sharpening blade and you will be surprised at how long it will continue to perform well. If you are not planning to use the blade right away, give it a light coating of silicone spray and wrap it in a protective covering. The package the blade came in is a good storage wrapper. Store unused circular saw blades in a safe place to keep them sharp and ready for service.

Reciprocating Saw Blades

Power tools in the reciprocating saw blade group include the ever popular *saber saw* (the first power saw most do-it-yourselfers buy, and according to industry statistics, the biggest selling saw of all) and the more rugged and heavy-duty reciprocating action saw. The major differences between these two saws are in power and cutting length. The standard home-owner's saber saw generally does not cut deeper than about 2″, while the heavy-duty type can have a blade 6″ to 8″ long.

Courtesy of Woodcraft Supply Corp

Store your circular saw blades carefully.

Sharpening Reciprocating Saw Blades

Sharpening all types of reciprocating saw blades is approached in the same manner, with a suitable three-sided slim taper file. It is important to choose a file that is not too wide for sharpening or damage to the teeth will occur. As a rule, most woodworkers do not sharpen reciprocating saw blades, but instead discard the dull blade and replace with a new one as needed. Although this approach may quickly solve the problem of a dull blade, it is wasteful, as these blades can be sharpened with just a little careful work with a file. If you are in the habit of discarding used reciprocating saw blades, consider saving a few and try sharpening them at your leisure. Once you have successfully sharpened one blade, you will be sorry that you ever threw one away.

All reciprocating saw blades are sharpened in the same manner. First, remove the blade from the power tool and sandwich it between two pieces of hardwood so that the gullets between the teeth are just above the hardwood. Next, clamp this unit in a bench vise so that the blade and hardwood are on a horizontal plane. If all teeth are the same height, jointing is not necessary. If some teeth are lower than others, however, run a flat file or sharpening stone over the tops of all teeth to make them all the same height. Using a suitable slim taper file, begin filing the tooth faces at about 8° right and left, or to the original angle and bevel of the teeth. As a guide, the teeth at the back end of the blade (where it is fastened into the saw) rarely show any signs of wear and can be used as a filing guide. File all teeth carefully and in a few minutes you will have a perfectly sharp reciprocating saw blade.

Handsaws

Undoubtedly, the most common hand-powered cutting tool in the home workshop is the handsaw. In this category we will find a variety of saws, including

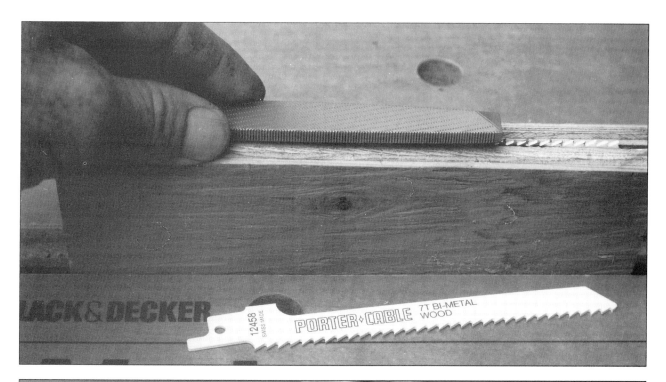

(Top photo) Jointing a reciprocating saw blade sandwiched between two pieces of lumber so the teeth are
just above the top.

(Above) Raise the teeth up to a comfortable working
height for filing.

coping, crosscut, dovetail, finish and keyhole saws, hacksaws and ripsaws. To be sure, there is an apparent trend to grab an electrically powered saw for a cutting task rather than a muscle-powered tool, but on those occasions where you have the time, you will find hand sawing a rewarding experience. It should be noted that fine-edged and straight cuts are the rule when a sharp handsaw is used for a cutting task. If time permits, cutting with a handsaw is one of those woodworking joys that some people look forward to—this author included.

Another reason for using a hand-powered saw for a cutting task might be that electrical power may not be readily available, although with the availability of portable electrical generating equipment, you can usually find a convenient source of power even for distant projects.

One other reason for choosing a handsaw might be the pure and simple satisfaction that is attached to work of this nature. Without the noise and bulk of power tools, you are able to feel closer to the work and therefore are in a better position to be one with the work. The end result, as anyone who knows will testify, is a project that you have even more reason to be proud of.

This may be a good time to review some of the basics of handsaw design. It is certainly no secret that part of the reason many of us do not use a handsaw is largely because we are unfamiliar with its capabilities. We can all benefit from a brief discussion of what makes a good handsaw.

What to Look for in a Handsaw

To begin with, any saw is only as good as the material and workmanship that goes into making it. A high-quality handsaw will be made of special steel, for this is one of the distinguishing marks of any select tool. Steel used in saw making must be durable—in this case, hard and tough—in order to hold a cutting edge. In addition, it must also be sturdy enough to

withstand buckling. In better saw steel, this is accomplished through metallurgically tempering special steel to an exact degree. The end result is an extremely tough saw that will hold an edge through long periods of use while at the same time having the right amount of resilience to withstand buckling yet permit proper filing and setting of the individual teeth.

It is probably safe to say that most handsaws are taper ground. This tapers the entire blade from teeth to back, so that the blade resembles an inverted wedge. The *kerf*—sometimes called the *cut*—made by the teeth is wide enough to permit the body of the saw to fit easily, reducing the natural tendency of the saw to bind or buckle.

One last thing to consider when answering the question "what makes a good handsaw" is the shape and positioning of the handle, for this has an effect on how well the saw performs. The handle should be designed to direct the saw's energy straight to the cutting teeth and not against the back of the saw. A

A handsaw provides a means of cutting when power is not available or for small cutting tasks.

well-positioned handle will not strain the wrist and will, in fact, make every ounce of your sawing energy count.

When shopping for a new handsaw, there are several points that you should check with the saw in hand:

Tension. To check the tension of a saw, flex it slightly and place a straightedge across the blade. The gap between the straightedge and saw blade should form a perfect arch. A lopsided bow indicates a poorly balanced saw.

Teeth. Hold the saw at arm's length. Bend the blade slightly to bring the points of the teeth into view along the breast of the blade. Points along the blade edge should all be the same length. Look along the flat sides of the blade and examine it for a uniform set. Poor setting of the teeth will cause the saw to cut inaccurately.

Finish. A quality handsaw should look and feel good. There should be no ridges, nicks or rough spots

A good handsaw should last for a lifetime.

along the blade. It is important to keep in mind that a smooth, highly polished finish will resist rust in addition to helping to cut down on friction when cutting. Even the handle on a quality handsaw will be finished well and be pleasing to both the hand and eye.

Using a Handsaw Correctly

As with most things in life, there is a right way and a wrong way to use a handsaw. For the benefit of those of you who may never have learned, let's quickly review how to properly use a handsaw. You will find hand sawing much easier when the saw is held correctly. When using a crosscut saw, for example, the saw wrist and forearm should form a straight line at an angle of 45° to the work. With a ripsaw, a steeper angle of about 60° is required for most efficient cutting. In either case, it is important always to keep your eye on the work and always to cut to the waste side of the work.

To start a cut, begin with a few short strokes, steadying the saw with the thumb of the free hand. Be extremely careful at this point, for there is a tendency for the blade to hop off the work, resulting in a cut hand or fingers. After a groove has been cut, continue sawing with long, steady strokes. Even strokes are easier on your hand and on the work. A short, jerky motion, in contrast, wastes energy and causes uneven tooth wear. Long, smooth strokes give faster cutting action and much better control. Use just enough pressure to keep the saw from chattering. By forcing the feed, you may upset the saw's balance. This is particularly true when cutting through a knot. Since the knot is much harder than the rest of the wood, it will call for slower—*not* faster—cutting speed action.

Support the waste end of the work with your free hand as the cut nears completion. Letting the waste end break off by itself often causes the work to split. Also guard against twisting the saw to knock off waste ends. This not only can ruin the tooth setting on the saw but possibly also break a tooth or two.

Properly cared for and treated, a good handsaw will last for many years. To ensure a long and useful life, there are a number of things that should be done to your handsaw in addition to keeping it sharp. First, keep a light coat of oil on all metal surfaces, either a light coat with a good silicone, such as WD-40, or a light coating of oil applied with a rag. This is the best insurance against surface rust. After using the saw, once again give it a light coat of silicone spray or oil. Get into the habit of doing this each and every time you use the saw and it will last a lifetime.

If you ever discover rust on your handsaw, try to remove it as quickly as possible. If the rust is just a light coating on the surface, often a quick wipe with an oily rag will remove it. However, if the rust has established a firm foothold, you must resort to more aggressive tactics. For removing medium to heavy rust, use an abrasive paper—emery cloth usually works well—and water. The usual technique is to wet the saw and place it rusty side up on a piece of dimensional lumber, such as a suitably sized piece of 2×8. Next, use emery cloth in conjunction with the water to rub the rust away. As you can well imagine, your work will be determined by the amount and depth of the rust you are removing. Circular motions work best, with the area kept wet by frequent applications of water. You may also find the addition of some valve grinding compound helpful. This abrasive paste is available from any automobile parts store. If nothing else, removing the rust from a favorite saw will be a lesson in keeping all handsaws—and other metal tools—lightly oiled in the future.

Sharpening a Handsaw

No matter how much loving care you give to your favorite handsaw, the fact remains that if you use it often, it will eventually lose its fine cutting edge, and you will notice that it requires more effort on your part to use. When this stage is reached there are only two real choices as to the best course of action. The first is to take the saw to a professional sharpening service and have them restore the cutting edge. Your second choice is, of course, to sharpen the handsaw yourself. It is probably safe to say that if you are in a hurry for the saw and have never sharpened a saw in the past, your best bet would be to have a professional do the sharpening. Keep in mind that the chances of ruining a good saw by improper sharpening are good if you do not have the time to learn how to accomplish this correctly. Some experts suggest that it is best to learn the basics of sharpening a handsaw on an old worthless saw. This way, if you make a few mistakes, you will not ruin a valuable saw. Then, once you have mastered the basics, you can apply these to your better handsaws.

Several things can be learned by carefully looking over a saw blade before attempting to sharpen it. The first part of your inspection should be to see if any teeth are broken or chipped. This can easily happen by hitting a nail or twisting the saw while cutting. Another possible source of damage to the saw might be as a result of rough handling in general, such as if the handsaw is kept in a large toolbox without some type of protective sheath over the blade. Whatever the cause, broken or missing teeth will indicate to you that more work will be required for the sharpening.

Sharpening of any handsaw is done in three steps: *jointing, fitting* and *setting.*

The first step in sharpening a handsaw is called *jointing,* an important step that makes all of the tips of the saw teeth the same height. If one tooth or more is broken, nicked or missing, you will have lots of work to do in getting all of the remaining unbroken teeth down to the same level.

The task of jointing a handsaw begins by first sandwiching the saw (teeth facing upward) between two pieces of scrap lumber. Clamp between the jaws of a bench vise so that the teeth of the saw protrude about ¾″ above the top edges of the lumber. This spacing is adequate for most people to work the saw teeth, but if your hands are larger or smaller than normal, you might find that increasing or decreasing the position of the teeth relative to the lumber will give you a more comfortable working height. The only caution that I can offer is that too much working height will not keep the saw blade stationary enough to work on efficiently. As a rule, if the saw blade moves or chatters during sharpening, reposition the blade lower into the wooden sandwich.

A professional saw sharpener uses a special tool for jointing a handsaw blade, but there is no need for the do-it-yourselfer to go to the extra expense. A flat file, when used with a sharp eye, can easily be used for jointing the teeth on a handsaw. Hold the file in both hands with the handle end of the file toward you. Hold your thumbs on the file, with your index fingers under the file and pointing toward you.

By holding the file in this manner it is easy to keep it at right angles to the sides of the saw. While filing, knuckles ride the "rails," such as they are, on the top edges of the lumber.

Push the file forward lightly over the saw lengthwise as many times as necessary to file all of the high points of the teeth down to the level of the lowest tooth. Some specialized lighting may be of help when jointing a handsaw with a file. By adjusting the lighting so that it shines on the teeth, it will be easy to see when all of the tips of the teeth have been touched by the file. This will appear as a bright flat plane on the top of each tooth. It will be easy to identify teeth that remain untouched after the file has made a few passes — they will look dull in color. Keep in mind that if any tooth is shorter than the rest, it will not do any cutting as the saw blade is pushed through a piece of lumber during the cutting process. Such a saw tooth is useless. Unless there has been some exceptional damage to one or more teeth on the blade, it should not take more than a

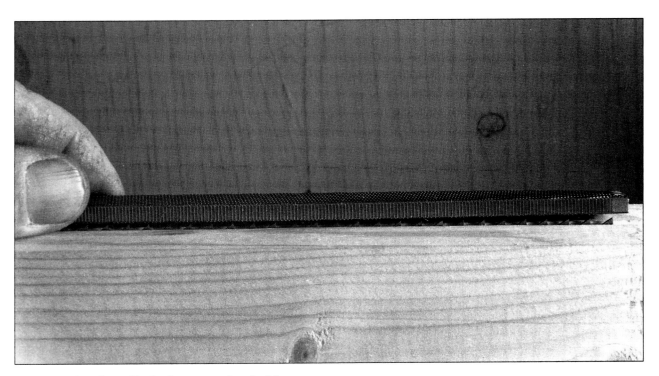

Jointing a handsaw blade that is sandwiched between two pieces of lumber.

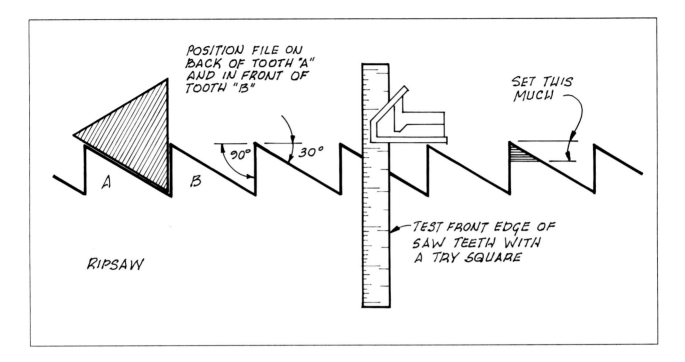

Filing angle for ripsaw teeth.

few passes with the file to render all teeth the same height.

The second step in the handsaw sharpening process is technically known as *fitting* the saw, but for simplicity's sake let's refer to this step as filing. Since there are two basically different tooth designs, ripsaw and crosscut saw, we must discuss each of these separately.

Storing a Handsaw

When not in use, a handsaw should be hung out of harm's way in the workshop. If you find it necessary to carry your handsaw around with other tools, cover the blade with some type of protective wrapping, such as the slipcase it was sold in, to prevent damage to the surface and teeth. Some traveling woodworkers like to keep all handsaws in a special handsaw carrying case. Although this special saw box is another thing to carry around, it also is the most long-lived storage for saws that one could ask for.

Ripsaw

The shape of ripsaw teeth is shown in the illustration above. The front or cutting face of the teeth is at right angles to an imaginary line drawn along the points of the teeth. You can easily check this with a square as shown in the illustration. A triangular file in the correct position is also shown. Also note that the side of the file that is against the front of a tooth is held plumb. By holding one side of the file plumb and by pressing the file down into the gullet, the back of the tooth will be at a 30° angle to a line along the points of the teeth.

Assuming that you are right-handed, hold the handle end of the file firmly; hold the point of the file lightly between the thumb and index finger of the left hand. File every other tooth from one side of the saw, then turn the saw end for end, and file the rest of the teeth from the other side in the same fashion. At each stroke, the file must cut the back of the tooth that projects away from you and the front of the adjoining tooth as well. If the teeth are uneven, they should be gradually equalized in size by pressing the file against the larger tooth.

The position of the saw during filing should be

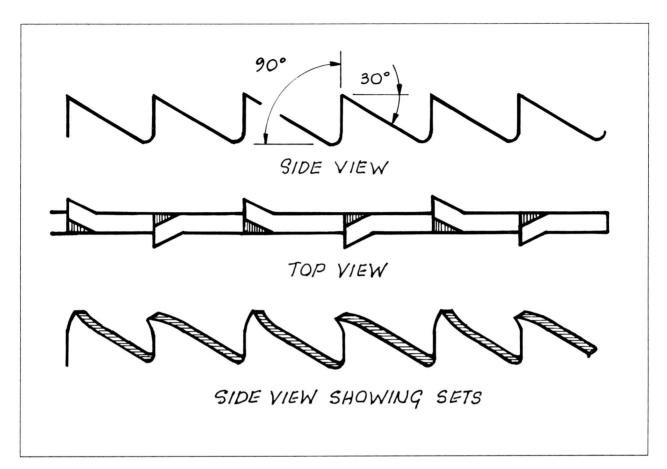

Angle for setting ripsaw teeth.

to your advantage, that is in an easy-to-work position. As a rule, place the saw in the wooden clamp so that the teeth protrude above by about ¾". If the saw vibrates or moves it is probably too high and must be lowered so that the file can be worked properly. Hold the file straight across the saw.

Since a file cuts on the forward stroke only, raise it at the end of each stroke and bring it back into a sharpening position. Long, light, even strokes of the file are the best way to ensure that the filing is done correctly. It is probably safe to estimate that the average ripsaw tooth can be sharpened with no more than two or three long strokes of a sharp file.

After a saw is filed, all of the teeth should be uniform. Sometimes, however, one or more teeth will have been filed incorrectly. It is important, therefore, to scrutinize each tooth after you feel that the filing has been completed. Refile any teeth that appear to

have been filed improperly before going on to the next step in the sharpening process.

The teeth of a ripsaw blade are really a series of tiny chisels. If all of the teeth are the same size, shape and height, each will cut with a force that is equal to the others and the cutting will go smoothly. Teeth that are not uniform, however, will cause the cutting action to be other than expected.

The final step in the sharpening of a ripsaw is called *setting* and this is done to make the kerf of the saw greater than the thickness of the blade. As a point of reference, a ripsaw to be used in wet or green wood operates much more efficiently if the kerf is wide. A ripsaw used on dry lumber, on the other hand, needs only the slightest kerf to cut well. Every other tooth is set to the right, and the rest of the teeth are set to the left. The easiest way of setting saw teeth is with a special, plier-like tool called a saw set. This tool is hand-operated and simply bends individual teeth outward to create the kerf.

Adjust the tool so that not more than half of each tooth is set, or in other words so that only the point and not the whole of each tooth is bent. As a point of reference, the shaded part of the tooth in the illustration on page 109 is bent with the saw set tool. Remember that the teeth are set left and right alternately along the entire length of the blade.

The illustration on page 109 is an enlarged view of the teeth of a ripsaw. You can easily see that the cutting edge of each tooth is square to the saw blade and that every other tooth is set to the right. Once again, remember that wet or green wood requires a ripsaw with a wider kerf than dry wood.

Crosscut Saw

As mentioned earlier, the teeth on a crosscut saw differ somewhat from those on a ripsaw, so they must be sharpened with a different approach. To begin with, crosscut teeth must be jointed to bring all of the tips of the teeth to the same plane or line, the same as the teeth of a ripsaw are jointed. The same technique can be used for jointing crosscut teeth as was used for ripsaw teeth—a flat file run horizontally over the tops of the teeth.

After jointing, the teeth of your crosscut saw may resemble those in the top illustration on page 111. Of the four teeth shown, the point of tooth 1 has just been touched by the file; tooth 2 was considerably longer and much of the tip has been filed away, leaving a large, flat surface; tooth 3, as a result of a poor previous filing, was also longer than tooth 1; and tooth 4 is larger than any of the others. To file these teeth properly, tooth 1 is left as is; tooth 2 is brought to a point by filing against the front edge only; the back of tooth 3 is filed with the same strokes of the file used for the front of tooth 2; and tooth 4 is brought to a point by filing the front and

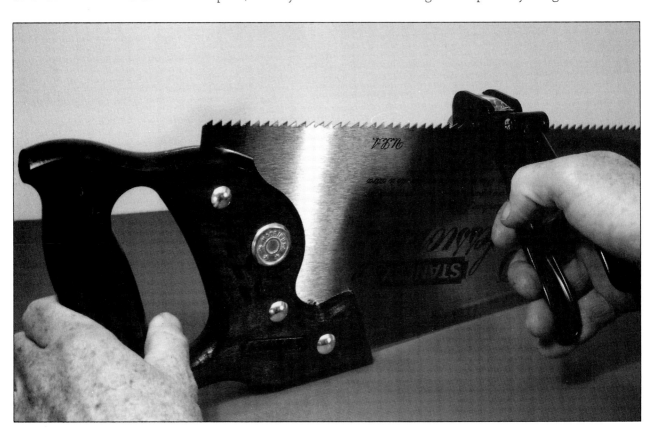

Use a tooth setting tool for setting handsaw teeth.

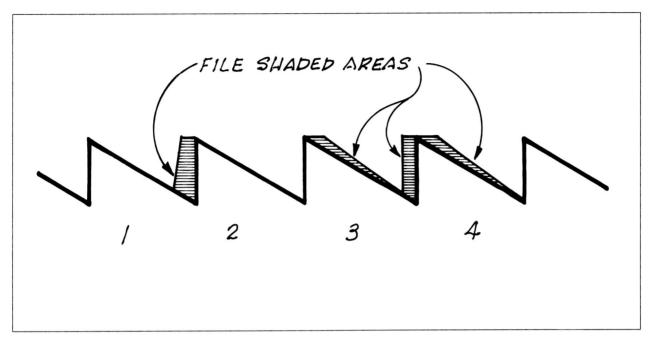

File the shaded areas of this crosscut saw.

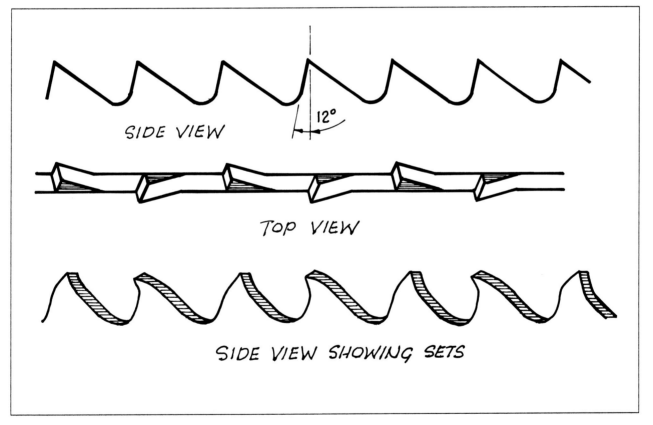

Crosscut teeth.

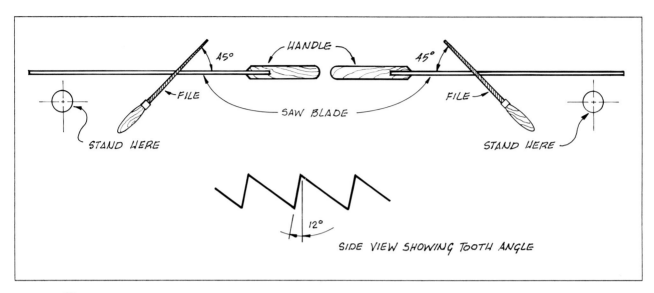

How to file a crosscut saw.

back edges until the metal is filed away to the dotted lines. By using this procedure, all the teeth are made equal — the same size and shape.

The correct shape of the teeth of a crosscut handsaw is shown in the bottom illustration on page 111. It should be noted that the front or cutting edge of each tooth is not at a right angle to the line of teeth, as the teeth on a ripsaw. The teeth on a crosscut saw are 12° more than a right angle, or 102°. This is an industry standard for crosscut saw teeth. If the cutting edges of the teeth were filed at a right angle, the saw would draw into the wood too much and the end result would be a rough cut.

The angle of a saw tooth is often referred to by professional sharpeners as the *hook* of a saw. The amount of hook of the teeth is controlled by the extent to which the file is tilted or tipped sideways toward the point of the tooth during filing. If the file were so held as to have its topside horizontal, the front and back of each tooth would have the same angle. There would not be enough hook to the front of the teeth to cause them to take hold and cut well. Such a saw is spoken of as a *peg-tooth* saw and, as you can easily guess, it will not cut well.

A crosscut handsaw blade is not filed straight across as the ripsaw was previously. Hold the file so

that the point of the file points toward the handle of the saw, and so that there is an angle of 45° between the handle end of the file and the tip end of the saw. The smaller this angle — that is, the closer the handle end of the file is held to the blade of the saw — the keener will be the resulting cutting edges of the teeth. There is a difference of opinion among the experts as to the best or most advantageous way to hold the file. Some of the pros file at a 45° angle, as described earlier, filing against the cutting edges of the teeth. Others file toward the tip of the saw and maintain that the saw takes hold better and makes a smoother cut. The 45° method I have described is the most popular and should provide totally acceptable results for you. The position in which the filer should stand is also indicated in the illustration. A filer may begin at either end and at either side and file every other tooth, then turn the saw in the vise and file all of the missed teeth in the same manner.

To ensure the best success, file very carefully, stopping often to examine the work as it progresses. If a watchful eye is kept, it is safe to assume that the filing will result in predictable results.

The last step in the sharpening process for a crosscut saw is setting the teeth. This is accomplished with a plier-like saw tooth setting tool in the same manner as used for setting ripsaw teeth. Tooth set makes the cut or kerf wider than the thickness of the blade. The amount of set depends largely on the type of work that will be done with the saw. As a rule, green or wet wood requires more set than dry woods do. For all-around general crosscut use, the saw teeth should be set a little wider than normal. The only possible exception to this is when using a crosscut saw for finish cutting of cabinet or other fine woodwork.

To be sure, there are other types of saws around the home workshop than those described above. Generally speaking, however, all straight saws fall into one of two categories — ripsaw or crosscut — so if you are faced with sharpening a straight saw, approach it from one of these points of reference and you will not go wrong.

This clamp-on filing guide will simplify handsaw sharpening.

CHAPTER ELEVEN
Sharpening Other Shop Tools

Many tools around the average home workshop get used with great frequency with little thought to their condition, other than being put back where they can be found—tools that we pretty much take for granted, such as screwdrivers, awls, scrapers, scissors and nail sets. In this chapter we will cover a multitude of common tools that can benefit from a little touching up. In the end, you will learn how to sharpen these tools to make them more effective for a given task and, of possible greater importance, extend their service life.

Sharpening Scissors

The average home has several pairs of scissors that are used for a variety of tasks and there is probably nothing quite as frustrating as a dull pair. They don't cut worth a darn and more often than not give a ragged edge to the material being cut. The blades of a good pair of scissors are not flat as they appear at first glance, but are instead concave. This design feature causes pressure to be exerted along the point of the cut as the scissors are opened and closed. This tension is further enhanced by the pivot screw.

As a rule, you should not sharpen scissors unless they are very dull. Often, simply tightening the pivot screw will give a marked improvement in how they cut, so try this before deciding to sharpen the edges.

The beveled cutting edges on a good pair of scissors are at an angle of approximately 80°. You can restore this easily with a fine-grained stone simply by stroking several times. Use some oil to help the honing and give your undivided attention to recreating the original bevel. The bevel must be consistent along the entire cutting edge. This will require careful work, especially for long-bladed shears. After a few swipes on each blade, clean off any oil, abrasive grit and metal deposits and then open and close the scissors several times. This action will remove the tiny wire edge that will have formed on the back (flat side) of the blades.

The next step is to make a test cut on heavy paper. This test will reveal if the bevels are true. A clean cut means that the sharpening was done correctly, but a ragged-edge cut means that the bevel is

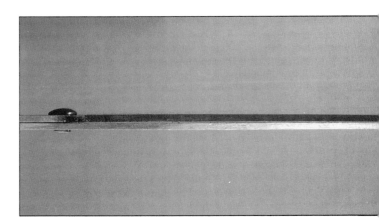

Scissor blades are concave, not flat.

inconsistent. Look over both blades carefully for the source of the problem and correct as necessary.

Scissors can also be sharpened on a stationary vertical sander, providing a dependable tool rest is available. The tool rest is necessary not only to steady the tool during sharpening but also to hold the blade at the proper angle for the edge bevel. Open the scissors as wide as they will go, then place on the edge guide. The belt should travel into the edge. Move the scissors into the belt at the proper bevel and make a quick pass, left to right or right to left. It is important that the scissors be kept in motion or a flat spot will result that will make the scissors useless and mean additional work to get them back in cutting shape. As a rule, a light touch is far better than trying to force the bevel on the sander. Grind the second blade in the same manner.

After sharpening scissors by either of the two methods described above, clean them with a dry cloth. It is important to remove any oil, abrasive grit or metal particles from the sharpening. Next, check the tension of the pivot screw and adjust if necessary. The last step is to apply a coat of clean, lightweight oil to all surfaces of the scissors. A good choice is 10W or a light application of silicone spray. Work this lubricating oil into the scissors by opening and closing them several times. Then take a clean, dry cloth and remove all of the oil. Now the scissors are ready for service.

The general sharpening procedures outlined will work with most types of scissors, but one exception is worth noting. If scissors have other than flat or straight cutting edges — serrated edges, for example — you must sharpen in a different manner. As a rule, special-edged scissors require a small or V-shaped stone for the sharpening task. Sharpen only the top edges of the irregular blade and not the shear faces. Work carefully and just sharpen up the angle of the bevel with the stone. Use a few drops of oil. After you have done the best you can on the bevel, make a few passes on the back of the blade to remove any

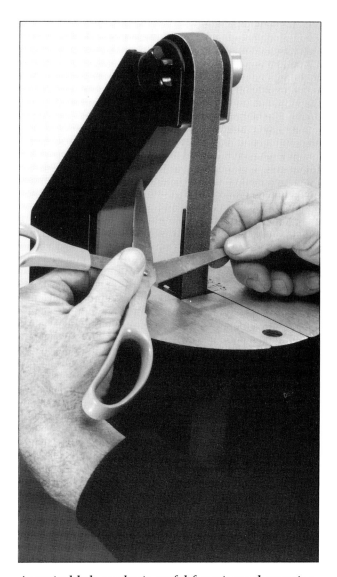

A vertical belt sander is useful for scissor sharpening.

feather edge that may have formed. Wipe the scissors clean with a dry cloth, removing all oil, grit and metal particles, then make a test cut. If you are not satisfied with the cutting action, adjust the pivot screw and this should correct the problem.

Both straight-edged and serrated-edged scissors can also be sharpened with the GATCO sharpening system. The professional set comes with three flat stones and one V-shaped stone for sharpening serrated-edged scissors and knives. The system is detailed in chapter two, Tools for Sharpening.

Sharpening Tin Snips

Metal-cutting tasks often pop up in the workshop — making metal templates, for example — and the best and easiest way to accomplish these is with a pair of tin snips. In addition to cutting sheet-type metals, tin snips are also handy for cutting other sheet-type materials such as cardboard, leather and upholstery fabric. Because they have heavy jaws, tin snips cut easily through materials that are impossible for a pair of scissors. Some tin snips are designed for straight cuts; others make right- or left-hand cuts.

Tin snips are similar to conventional scissors but are a much more heavy-duty tool. Like scissors, the small blades are concave in shape and are held together with a set screw or bolt and nut. The better types of tin snips are spring loaded so the jaws are always open, a feature that reduces hand fatigue when working on large cutting projects.

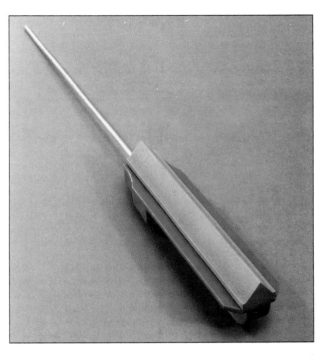

This GATCO stone is made for sharpening serrated tools.

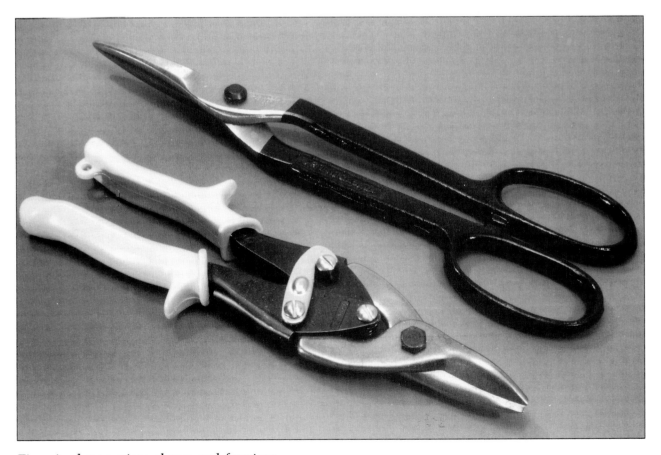

Tin snips have various shapes and functions.

Some tin snips have straight-edged blades while others have slightly serrated edges. Straight blades are best sharpened with a bench stone, file or stationary vertical sander, while serrated blades require either a fine slim-taper file or triangular whetstone. As a rule, both types of blades are best sharpened with a stone rather than a file or sander.

The blades on some models lend themselves to being disassembled, but this is not generally necessary unless extensive grinding to remove damage is required. Simply open the snips as far as they will go and work with a stone (and a few drops of honing oil) to reestablish a crisp 25° angle. After both blades have been honed, whet the flat or shear faces a few times to remove any fine wire that may have developed as a result of the sharpening.

After sharpening, wipe the blades with a clean, dry cloth to remove oil, grit and tiny bits of metal. Next turn your attention to the pivot screw or bolt. This fastener carries a heavy load when in use and proper tension is therefore important. Tighten the bolt to the point where the shear faces are held closely but not touching, except at the point of shearing as the blades are worked. After adjusting the pivot bolt, lubricate the snips with a lightweight machine oil or silicone spray, then wipe clean. It is important to lubricate the return spring and any pivot rivets in the handles. This will make the snips operate much more smoothly.

Most tin snips have a catch hook that holds the blades closed when not in use. This helps to keep the blades sharp during storage.

Sharpening Wire Cutters

Wire cutters are handy pliers used for cutting and stripping wire of all gauges and must therefore be sharp to work efficiently. As a rule, the cutting edges can easily be touched up with a stone, but if extensive damage has been sustained — commonly by cutting a live electrical wire — the area cannot be reground. When wire cutters have been damaged to this extent, you can only use them as is or discard them.

When sharpening wire cutters it is important to reestablish the original bevel of about 45° without removing too much metal. The innermost recess of

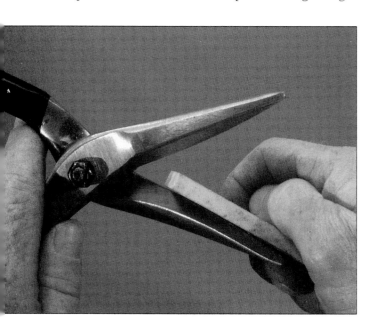

Stone the cutting edges of tin snips.

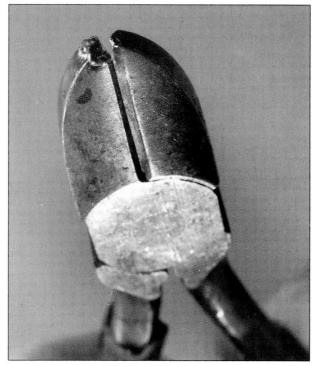

Wire cutters that are damaged should be discarded.

Use a small pocket stone to sharpen the cutting surfaces of wire cutters.

the jaws usually has the least amount of wear so you should check here for the bevel angle if you are uncertain.

Work carefully with a small stone, medium to fine grit, and do not remove more metal than is necessary to do the sharpening. After both cutting edges have been honed, lubricate the areas around which the jaws pivot, then wipe the cutters with a clean, dry cloth.

Sharpening a Nail Set

A nail set is indispensable around the workshop for precisely driving the heads of finish nails below the surface of the work. A nail set does not have a cutting edge like other tools but will work much more efficiently if touched up every so often. Because a nail set is struck by a hammer during use, both the top edge and tip often develop a burr or mushroom. These must be removed, as they have a tendency to

make an irregular hole when setting a nail and, of greater importance, can become a projectile if they should break off during use.

Begin by carefully inspecting the tip and head of the nail set. Chances are very good that you will discover a burr or mushroom on both ends of the tool. The best way to remove these is on a bench grinder. Work on the head of the nail set first to remove any mushrooming. A light touch into the spinning wheel should be all that is required to restore this area. As always when grinding, do not allow the tool to heat up, as the temper will be destroyed.

Next turn your attention to the nail set tip. While rotating the tool, touch the tip to the side of the grinding wheel. Keep twisting the tool as you lightly grind off any burr. Next touch the nail set tip to the face of the grinder. Exercise care here and do not form a point on the tip. It should be flat and square. Lastly, look over the tool and if you discover any

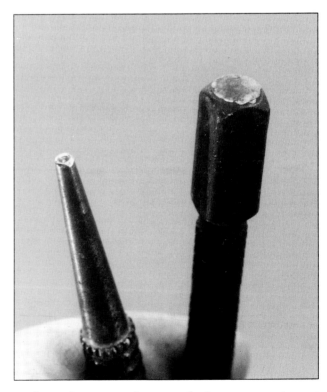

Nail sets have a tendency to mushroom over time at both the head and tip.

Carefully grind a nail set, rounding the head but keeping the tip flat.

burrs that may have formed while grinding, remove these with a flat file.

Sharpening an Awl

The distinguishing characteristic of the awl is that it is always tapered to a sharp point. An awl can be used for starting screw and nail holes, cleaning old paint from furniture, scribing cut lines on lumber and a variety of other tasks. An awl should not be used for setting nails, as the pointed tip tends to jump off the nail and will puncture the surrounding work.

As with any sharpening task, the first step is to look over the tool carefully to determine just how much work needs to be done. Since awl-like hand

tools are commonly used in conjunction with a hammer, the head of the tool must be inspected for mushrooming. The shaft may also be bent. In which case, use a bench vise to straighten it. If the tool has seen a lot of service, its head will probably be mushroomed over and this must be reground during the sharpening process. Your task is to restore the original bevel to the head of the tool and this is most easily accomplished by holding it against a bench grinder. Adjust the tool rest to the best advantage and remove all mushroomed metal from the head.

The next step is to sharpen the point on the tool, but first carefully look at the tip to determine if it is four-sided or cone-shaped. A four-point is most easily sharpened on a bench grinder, while a cone-shaped point is commonly sharpened with a medium or fine grit whetstone.

The four-sided point is most easily developed on a bench grinder. First adjust the tool rest (with the bench grinder off) so that when the shaft of the tool is rested on it, the angle of the grind will be approximately 35°. Next turn your bench grinder on, and once the spinning wheel has reached maximum rpm, lay the tool on the guide so that the tip just comes in contact with the wheel. Grind for a few moments, then remove the tool from the tool rest. Now turn the tool over so that the first grind is on top and grind the opposite side of the point. Remove the tool and you should have two flat surfaces on opposite sides of the point. The next two grinds should be done so that when finished you have ground four flat sides, forming a point on the end of the tool. Keep in mind that the tip of the tool should never become too hot to touch. To prevent this, dip the tool into a container of water after each side has been ground. The end result should be a four-sided point.

To achieve a cone-shaped point on an awl, you will find a whetstone helpful. First apply a few drops of oil to the surface of the stone, then turn the tool between your fingers while at the same time stroking it along the stone, holding the shaft and tilting it up to form the desired point angle. Keep turning the tool so that the point remains in the center of the tool. If, for example, you were to stroke several times without twisting the tool, the point would move off center. Inspect the work often. When the desired point is achieved, wipe off the oil and the tool is ready for service.

Sharpening Screwdrivers

The well-equipped home workshop will have a good selection of screwdrivers, both flat-bladed and Phillips. To be effective, the tip of a flat-bladed screwdriver must be square and should fit snugly into a screw slot. More often than not, when a screwing task is at hand, the first screwdriver available is the one that gets used. Just as often, the tip of the screwdriver does not fit well into the screw slot and the end results are commonly a stripped screw head, skinned knuckles and a poor overall job. The need for choosing a properly fitting screwdriver from the three or four that are common in most workshops

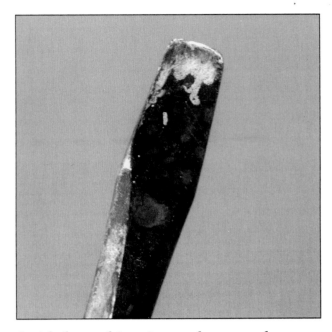

A nicked screwdriver tip must be reground.

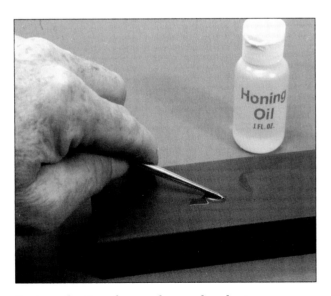

Restore the tip of an awl on a bench stone; use lubricant.

is important for success. In addition, the more the tip of a screwdriver is used, the greater the chances of it becoming rounded or chipped and thus much less effective.

If a flat-bladed screwdriver becomes rounded or nicked in the tip, this damage must be repaired on a bench grinder. Begin by adjusting the tool rest so that the end of the screwdriver can be ground off at a perfect 90° angle to the shaft of the tool. Do not let the screwdriver become too hot to touch or the temper of the metal will be destroyed. It will become brittle and break easily during use. Keep a can of water next to the bench grinder and dip the tool into this often to keep the temperature down.

After the tip of the screwdriver has been squared off, the next step is to make the two flat sides of the tip parallel for about 1/16" to 1/4". This is done by holding the screwdriver by the shank and pressing lightly into the side of the grinding wheel. Grind one side, then repeat the grinding on the other flat side of the tip. When you are finished, the tip should be square at the end and the two flat sides, behind the tip, should be parallel.

Phillips screwdrivers also require touching up periodically or they will jump out of a screw slot easily. The best way to clean up the tip of a Phillips screwdriver is on a bench stone. First add a few drops of oil to the face of the stone. Then hold the shaft of the screwdriver at the proper bevel angle and make a few passes over the stone, while at the same time keeping the flat pressed firmly on the stone. Repeat this technique on all four flats of the tip. Work carefully; don't remove any more metal than is required for dressing up the edge.

As a rule, if the tip of a Phillips screwdriver has been chipped or extensively damaged, it is better to discard the tool and purchase a new one rather than try to regrind the tip. Broken Phillips screwdrivers can instead be reground to a point and pressed into service as an awl or in the garden as a weed digger.

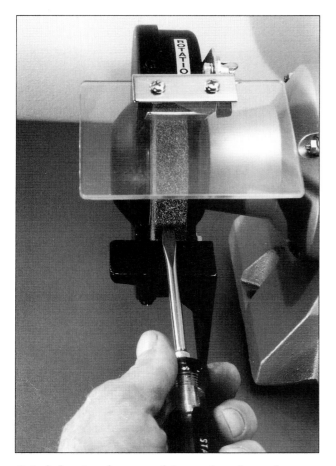

Grind the tip of a screwdriver using the tool rest, grinding at a 90° angle.

Sharpening Scrapers

Several types of scrapers can be found around the average home woodworking shop. There is, of course, the traditional scraper, which resembles a putty knife or joint knife, and there are also paint scrapers of several different varieties. As a rule, all scrapers operate by removing a thin layer of material from the surface of the work. Where there are differences between types of scrapers, they are generally along the lines of whether the tool is pulled or pushed across the surface of the work.

Generally, a scraper that is pulled across the surface will have a beveled edge, usually around 45°. On the other hand, scrapers that are pushed across the work surface commonly have a leading edge that is at a right angle to the blade — in short, square.

The tool size has some bearing on the method used to sharpen the scraper. Small scrapers usually can be sharpened quite easily with the aid of a good file, while larger scrapers can be touched up more quickly on a bench grinder. If the edge of the scraper is damaged (no matter what the edge type), it will have to be ground to a point just beyond the damage. This is most easily done on a bench grinder.

For scrapers with a flat edge, I find a file to be most useful for restoring the squareness. Probably the best example of a square-edge scraper is a paint scraper or putty knife. Most do-it-yourselfers do not know that a paint scraper has a square edge, and as a result put a beveled edge on this tool. Not only is this a waste of time (for this is not an easy task), but a paint scraper so sharpened will have a definite tendency to gouge the surface rather than take a layer of paint off. For future reference, the proper edge on a paint scraper is flat or 90°.

Probably the easiest way to put a square edge back on a paint scraper is to lay a file on the work bench or clamp it horizontally in a good vise. Next, with two hands, work the scraper over the file. It is important that the hands hold the scraper at a perfect

90° angle to the surface of the file. Of course, if the blade was damaged to begin with, it will have first been ground on a bench grinder, then worked with the file to achieve a 90° angled edge.

Beveled scrapers can be sharpened with either a bench grinder or file. Of course, if damage is present on the leading edge of this type of scraper, it must be ground past the damage and a new bevel then ground. If you find that grinding is necessary, work carefully and do not allow the metal to get too hot. Use the tool rest to aid in first grinding a 90° flat face, then adjust to the proper 35° finish edge. Generally speaking, a scraper blade need not be worked with a whetstone, for this would give a sharp edge that is not correct for this type of tool.

Sharpening a Pocketknife

I attended a woodworking shop seminar recently and was amazed when someone asked if anyone in the audience had a pocketknife handy. Out of about twenty attendees, at least twelve produced a Swiss officer's knife. Because of the popularity of pocketknives, particularly this type, I thought it would be helpful to explain how to sharpen one in this section. This information is not meant to duplicate the extensive coverage of knife sharpening found in chapter five. There you will learn how to regrind a damaged blade and restore a cutting edge to all types of carving knives. This section is simply intended to help you sharpen the tool that many of us carry every day.

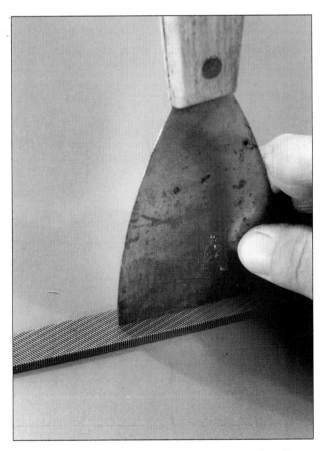

Square off the edge of a scraper using a flat file.

A vertical belt sander is useful for sharpening and squaring a scraper.

The best way to sharpen a pocketknife is on a combination bench stone (coarse/medium grit). Then finish off the sharpening with a fine-grained stone. Begin by placing a few drops of honing oil on the face of the stone, coarse side up. Next, holding the opened knife by the handle, begin stroking the stone. The cutting edge can be either leading or trailing. During the sharpening process, hold the blade at a consistent angle to form the bevel. For most general types of cutting — the type of cutting usually done with a pocketknife — a 15° bevel is about right.

Approximately twenty strokes per side should be all that is required to develop an edge on all but the dullest of pocketknives. The accepted technique is to make one pass over the stone, turn the blade over, and make another pass in the opposite direction. For example, if the first stroke is toward you, turn the blade over and push it away on the second stroke. During the entire length of the stroke, it is imperative to hold the blade at the 15° angle to develop a consistent bevel. This is simple for the straight part of the blade, but more difficult as you near the tip and the blade curves. For this part of the blade, lift up slightly to develop the same bevel around the tip.

After you have made about twenty passes over the coarse side of the stone, turn the stone over and repeat the process on the medium side. Use honing oil and maintain the same bevel, 15°. Another twenty passes over this side of the stone should produce a fairly sharp cutting edge on the average pocketknife. You may want to hone this edge to razor keenness by now switching to a fine grit stone and repeating the same process — twenty strokes held at a 15° bevel. This last honing will produce the sharpest of all cutting edges on a pocketknife.

If you are having problems sharpening a pocketknife or it is damaged and requires regrinding, please turn back to chapter five. There you will find a much more detailed discussion of knife sharpening as well as information on sharpening aids for knives.

Use a bench stone for knife sharpening.

CHAPTER TWELVE
Tool Storage Projects

Proper tool storage will do much to prevent damage to the working edges of tools. Obviously, a wood chisel stands a much greater chance of suffering damage to the cutting edge if it is simply left lying around the workshop or thrown in a toolbox. This chapter covers a few solutions to storing woodworking bits and cutters. You will also find a few woodworking projects that are fun to make and will make tools for sharpening more efficient to use.

Router Bit Storage Trays

Router bits have a tendency to get thrown in a box or drawer around the workshop and this commonly

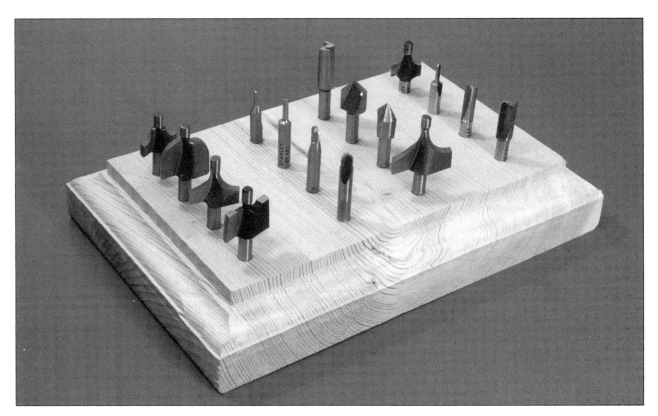

Small diameter router bit tray with top decorative edge.

Large capacity router bit tray with bottom decorative edge.

results in chips and other damage to them. One good solution is to make a wooden tray that holds individual cutters and protects them during storage.

When making a router bit storage tray, make it larger than you think you may need, that is to say with a capacity greater than the number of bits you now have on hand. That way, when you acquire more bits, you will have ample room to store them.

A simple but effective router bit tray can easily be made from a 12″ to 14″ long piece of dimensional lumber. For ½″ shaft router bits I use 1″ × 8″ lumber, and for ¼″ shaft bits I use 1″ × 6″ lumber. Choose a piece that is free of knots and straight grained.

For a decorative edge, use your router, fitted with an ogee bit, to run around all outside edges. For small router bit trays I run the router around the top edge, but for larger trays I decorate the bottom edge. Bottom decoration makes it easier to pick up and carry larger trays.

Once the edges have been worked, mark the top for drilling. For ¼″ router bits, evenly space these holes about 1″ to ½″ apart. For ½″ router bits, make the holes 2½″ apart. All holes should be evenly spaced in rows across the entire top.

Finish off the tray by sanding all surfaces and giving it two coats of clear finish. Trays like these should last a lifetime and provide safe storage for your router bits.

Shaper Cutter Rack

Shaper cutters can be damaged easily if not stored properly. A simple rack is ideal for preventing shaper cutter damage during storage. The rack also allows me to quickly choose the cutter I need for a given project.

The shaper cutter rack illustrated is made from a 10″ square piece of ¾″ A-B plywood. The back leg is a triangle 8″ high and will hold the stand steady.

Begin by cutting the two pieces of plywood. Next measure and mark holes on the face for ½″ wooden dowels. The holes should be spaced 3″ apart in three rows. Next, using a Forstner drill bit, drill about ⅝″ at each hole mark. Fasten the back support through the face of the stand. If you prefer, you can eliminate this rear support and wall hang the unit close to your shaper.

Cut nine pieces of ½″ wooden dowel, each 4″ long. Sand the ends to round slightly. Insert the dowels in the holes, using woodworker's glue to hold them in place. Finish off the shaper cutter rack with a coat of clear finish.

Forstner Bit Storage Rack

Forstner bits can be damaged easily and therefore should be stored carefully to protect their thin cutting edges. I have designed a rack that will store up to six Forstner bits (see photo, top right).

To make a Forstner bit storage rack, begin by

Forstner bit rack.

cutting three pieces from 1″ × 6″ clear pine or other suitable lumber. The ends measure 5½″ and the shelf is 7″ long. Make a dado cut ¾″ wide, ⅜″ deep and ¾″ up from the bottom on one side of both end pieces. Next measure and mark holes on the shelf. These should be 1½″ apart in two rows on the shelf top. Bore six holes ⅜″ in diameter and ½″ deep at the hole mark indications.

Lightly sand the rack and assemble by inserting the shelf into the end dado cuts. Use woodworker's glue and drive three No. 4 finish nails through each end and into the shelf. After the glue dries, give two coats of clear finish.

Woodworking Chisel Tray

Woodworking chisels can be damaged so easily that they never should be allowed to lay around the workshop unprotected. Although tip protectors are available (and in fact come attached to new, good chisels), woodworking chisels should be stored out of harm's way except when not actually in use. The chisel tray project here offers excellent protection for up to six chisels.

Shaper cutter rack.

Material List

1 — 20″ × 10″ × ¾″ A-B plywood — bottom (a)

1 — 20″ × 1″ × ¾″ pine — tip-holding rack (b)

1 — 20″ × 1″ × ¼″ A-A plywood — cover for tip rack (c)

2 — 20½″ × 2″ × ¼″ A-A plywood — sides (d)

2 — 10″ × 2″ × ¼″ A-A plywood — ends (e)

Begin by cutting all pieces according to the material list given. Next the tip-holding rack must be dado cut on either a table saw or with a router. Mark the piece (b) for dado cuts ½″ deep, 1″ wide and spaced 2″ apart. This is the most difficult part of the project, so work carefully. After the tip rack has been dado cut, the chisel tray can be quickly assembled.

Start by attaching the tip rack (b) along one edge of the bottom (a). Use woodworker's glue and finishing nails. Next attach the cover (c) over the tip rack with glue and wire brads. Last, assemble the sides (d) and the ends (e) of the unit in the same manner. After the glue dries, apply two coats of clear finish.

This chisel rack project will securely hold up to six standard size woodworking chisels. If you have long woodworking chisels (longer than 9″), increase the width of the project accordingly.

Woodworking chisel tray.

Sharpening Bench Stone Holder

The basic sharpening bench stone will provide years of service with just a minimum of care. Unfortunately, the smaller bench stones can be difficult and even dangerous to work with as there is little protection for your fingers during use. One good solution is to make a wooden base that will allow you to hold a sharpening stone without any risk of cutting yourself. A totally serviceable wooden base can be made from a scrap piece of lumber, but a much more attractive and functional base can be made from a piece of hardwood.

The illustrated bench stone base is for a stone that measures 4¼″ × 1¾″ × ½″. If your bench stone is larger or smaller, make suitable adjustments. Generally speaking, the base should be about 1″ wider and 2″ longer than the stone in hand.

Cut a hardwood block (in this case 2½″ × 6¼″ × 1½″) to size. Then trace the outline of the sharpening stone onto the top of the block. The sharpening stone should be centered on the block before tracing its outline. Next, using a ½″ straight router bit, remove material from inside the lines. Set your router so that when you have routed the position for the stone, it will be ¼″ higher than the base. Since this operation must be done freehand, make certain that the block is securely fastened and will not move. After routing, check the fit of the sharpening stone in the center of the base. If necessary, remove more wood at the corners with a chisel to square the area.

Next, using a Roman ogee router bit, put a decorative edge around the top of the block. Once you are satisfied with the fit of the stone — it should be reasonably snug — and its outside decoration, apply a coat of linseed oil to the block and your sharpening stone base is ready for service.

Wooden File Handles

Although both plastic and wooden handles are available, the most common way of purchasing files is without a handle. It is easy to solve this problem by making file handles in the home workshop. The simplest of all file handles are made from wooden dowels. Use ¾" diameter wooden dowels for all but the largest files and rasps. Each handle should be approximately 4" long.

After cutting a dowel to the desired length, drill a suitable hole in one end to accommodate the tang end of a file. For small files, a hole of about ⅛" diameter is suitable, but for larger files you will probably require a hole of ¼" or larger in diameter. After a hole has been drilled in one end, round off the other end with sandpaper. Then lightly sand the entire handle for smoothness.

To really finish off your custom file handles, give them a coat of acrylic paint. This will protect the wood, and if you use different color paints, will help you to identify specific files, such as red paint for triangular files and blue paint for flat files.

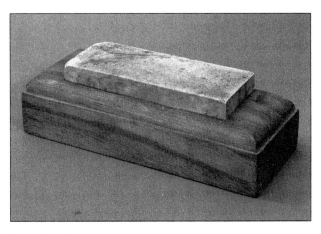

Base for bench stone.

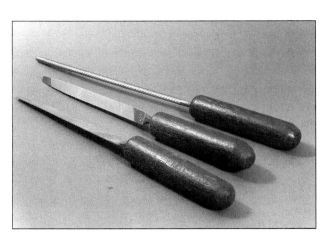

Wooden file handles.

GLOSSARY

Abrasive — Any man-made or natural material commonly used for sharpening, grinding or polishing metal.

Arbor — The rotating shaft of a motor or sharpening device onto which an abrasive or polishing wheel is bolted.

Back — The part of a blade or tooth that does not do the actual cutting.

Bevel — The inclined surface behind the cutting or leading edge of a tool (e.g., knife, chisel, plane iron, etc.)

Bevel Angle — The degree of incline that is the result of grinding the leading edge of a tool back to form a cutting edge.

Burnish — To polish by rubbing with an abrasive material until a mirrorlike finish appears.

Burr — A wire edge that is formed when a tool is ground or worked on an abrasive surface during the sharpening process.

Carbide — A compound of an element, usually metal, with carbon, which results in an extremely hard material. Silicon carbide is used for abrasive wheels and stones; tungsten carbide is used for tool edges.

Carbide Tip — A small piece of tungsten carbide welded to a tool edge that becomes the cutting edge.

Tungsten carbide is much harder than tool steel and therefore does not wear as much during use.

Carbon — An element that, when combined with iron, forms various kinds of steel. In steel it is the changing carbon content that determines the physical properties of the steel.

Chip — Damage to a cutting edge where a tiny section has been removed or has fallen away.

Concave — Having a surface that is hollowed or rounded inward.

Convex — Having a surface that curves or bulges outward, like a ball.

Cut — *See* **kerf**.

Cutting Angle — The degree of a cutting edge measured between a line perpendicular to the surface being cut and the face side of the tool. Also known as **rake**.

Drawknife — Used for roughing work on timber and lumber prior to construction. Also known as **drawshare**.

Dress — To restore the face of a grinding wheel using a special cutter wheel that breaks the glaze on the surface.

Edge — The leading part of a tool that does the actual

cutting of material.

Face — The front or leading edge of a cutting edge (blade, tooth, etc.) that does the cutting and that is sharpened.

File Card — A special brush used for file cleaning.

Flute — The channel-like straight or spiral groove of a cutter or bit that removes chips from a hole or cut.

Glaze — To become glossy or smooth as a result of metal particle buildup.

Grind — To wear away a surface by rubbing with a harder material.

Grinder — A device, commonly powered by an electric motor, used to spin an abrasive wheel.

Grit — An industrial classification standard that describes the size of abrasive grains or granules. Grit sizes are standard for abrasive paper, stones and wheels.

Gullet — The opening in front of a saw tooth or cutter that carries chips or sawdust out of the cut.

Hollow Ground — Bevel-ground to form a concave surface, rather than a flat plane.

Hone — The final sharpening on a fine grit abrasive stone or butcher's steel that results in the keenest possible cutting edge.

Honing Oils — The many oils offered by sharpening stone manufactuers; probably the best stone lubricant for sharpening.

Hook — The angle of a saw tooth.

Joint — The process of making all teeth on a saw blade the same height by filing their tops.

Kerf — The cutting path or groove made by a saw blade in wood or metal. Sometimes called **cut**.

Lap — The actual cutting edge of a drill bit or boring tool.

Nick — Damage to a cutting edge resulting from stress in the metal or from striking a harder material.

Pitch — The resinous material (sap) present in all woods that adheres to cutting tools and causes them to heat up excessively.

Quench — To cool warm or hot metal by immersing in water, oil or special cooling liquid.

Rake — (*see* **Cutting Angle**).

Secondary Bevel — An additional bevel formed just behind the leading edge of a sharpened tool to support and strengthen it.

Set — The alternate outward bending of steel saw teeth that results in a saw kerf that is wider than the thickness of the blade.

Shank — The shaft of a rotary bit or tool that is held in the chuck of the tool and that does no cutting or boring.

Slip stone — A small hand-held abrasive stone, most commonly in the fine grit sizes, that is used for final honing of cutting edges. Slip stones come in curved as well as flat shapes.

Spur — A sharp point or edge of a rotary cutting tool or bit that is designed to tear cross-grained wood fibers.

Strop — To add a final keenness to a cutting edge by stroking with leather, with the cutting edge trailing.

Temper — The correct heat treatment of a metal tool, particularly the cutting edge, to produce the desired degree of hardness.

Tool Rest — That part of a machine on which a tool is supported during grinding or use.

Tool Steel — Steel that has been alloyed with any of

a variety of elements to make it harder.

Try Square — An instrument used to test whether work is square.

Whet — To rub a tool's cutting edge on or over an abrasive surface to form a keen edge. *Also known as* **Hone**.

Whetstone — A fine-grit abrasive that is used to wear away a cutting edge during sharpening after the edge has been ground or otherwise worn away with a coarse abrasive.

Wire Edge — The fine, slightly curved burr that is formed during the final sharpening process.

INDEX

More Great Books for Your Woodshop!

Build Your Own Router Tables—Increase your router's accuracy, versatility and usefulness with a winning table design. Detailed plans and instructions for three types of tables plus a variety of specialty jigs and fixtures will help you create the right table for your shop. *#70367/$21.99/160 pages/300 illus./paperback*

The Encyclopedia of Joint Making—Create the best joints for every project! This comprehensive resource shows you how to prepare lumber, prevent layout errors, select the right joint, choose the best fastener and more. *#70356/$22.99/144 pages/300+ color illus.*

The Woodworker's Guide to Furniture Design—Discover what it takes to design visually pleasing and comfortably functional furniture. Garth Graves shows you how to blend aesthetics and function with construction methods and material characteristics to develop designs that really work! *#70355/$27.99/208 pages/110 illus.*

Build Your Own Entertainment Centers—Now you can customize the construction and design of an entertainment center to fit your skill level, tools, style and budget. With this heavily illustrated guidebook, you'll explore the whole process—from selecting the wood to hardware and finishing. *#70354/$22.99/128 pages/paperback*

Good Wood Finishes—Take the mystery out of one of woodworking's most feared tasks! With detailed instructions and illustrations you'll learn about applying the perfect finish, preparing materials, repairing aged finishes, graining wood and much more. *#70343/$19.99/128 pages/325+ color illus.*

Measure Twice, Cut Once, Revised Edition—Miscalculation will be a thing of the past when you learn these effective techniques for checking and adjusting measuring tools, laying out complex measurements, fixing mistakes, making templates and much more! *#70330/$22.99/144 pages/144 color illus.*

100 Keys to Woodshop Safety—Make your shop safer than ever with this manual designed to help you avoid potential pitfalls. Tips and illustrations demonstrate the basics of safe shopwork—from using electricity safely and avoiding trouble with hand and power tools to ridding your shop of dangerous debris and handling finishing materials. *#70333/$17.99/64 pages/125 color illus./paperback*

Making Elegant Gifts From Wood—Develop your woodworking skills and make over 30 gift-quality projects at the same time! You'll find everything you're looking to create in your gifts—variety, timeless styles, pleasing proportions and imaginative designs that call for the best woods. Plus, technique sidebars and hardware installation tips make your job even easier. *#70331/$24.99/128 pages/30 color, 120 b&w illus.*

Getting the Very Best From Your Router—Get to know your router inside and out as you discover new jigs and fixtures to amplify its capabilities, as well as techniques to make it the most precise cutting tool in your shop. Plus, tips for comparing different routers and bits will help you buy smart for a solid long-term investment. *#70328/$22.99/144 pages/225+ b&w illus.*

Good Wood Handbook, 2nd Edition—Now you can select and use the right wood for the job—before you buy. You'll discover valuable information on a wide selection of commercial softwoods and hardwoods—from common uses, color and grain to how the wood glues and takes finish. *#70329/$19.99/128 pages/250 color illus.*

100 Keys to Preventing & Fixing Woodworking Mistakes—Stop those mistakes before they happen—and fix those that have already occurred. Numbered tips and color illustrations show you how to work around flaws in wood; fix mistakes made with the saw, plane, router and lathe; repair badly made joints, veneering mishaps and finishing blunders; assemble projects successfully and more! *#70332/$17.99/64 pages/125 color illus.*

Build Your Own Mobile Power Tool Centers—Learn how to "expand" shop space by building mobile workstations that maximize utility, versatility and accessibility of woodshop tools and accessories. *#70283/$19.99/144 pages/250 b&w illus./paperback*

Creating Your Own Woodshop—Discover dozens of economical ways to fill unused space with the woodshop of your dreams. Self shows you how to convert space, lay out the ideal woodshop, or improve your existing shop. *#70229/$18.99/128 pages/162 b&w photos/illus./paperback*

Tables You Can Customize—Learn how to build four types of basic tables—from a Shaker coffee table to a Stickley library table—then discover how to apply a wide range of variations to customize the pieces to fit your personal needs. *#70299/$19.99/128 pages/150 b&w illus./paperback*

The Woodworker's Sourcebook, 2nd Edition—Shop for woodworking supplies from home! Self has compiled listings for everything from books and videos to plans and associations. Each listing has an address and telephone number and is rated in terms of quality and price. *#70281/$19.99/160 pages/50 illus.*

The Stanley Book of Woodworking Tools, Techniques and Projects—Become a better woodworker by mastering the fundamentals of choosing the right wood, cutting tight-fitting joints, properly using a marking gauge and much more. *#70264/$19.95/160 pages/400 color illus./paperback*

Good Wood Routers—Get the most from your router with this comprehensive guide to hand-held power routers and table routing. You'll discover a world of information about types of routers, their uses, maintenance, setup, precision table routing and much, much more. *#70319/$19.99/128 pages/550 color illus.*

Tune Up Your Tools—Bring your tools back to perfect working order and experience safe, accurate cutting, drilling and sanding. With this handy reference you'll discover how to tune up popular woodworking machines, instructions for aligning your tools, troubleshooting charts and many other tips. *#70308/$22.99/144 pages/150 b&w illus./paperback*

Desks You Can Customize—Customize your furniture to fit your personal style. With Graves's instruction and detailed drawings, you'll create a unique, individualized desk as you experiment with legs, doors, drawers, organizers and much more. *#70309/$19.99/128 pages/133 b&w illus./paperback*

Make Your Woodworking Pay for Itself, Revised Edition—Find simple hints for selling your work to generate a little extra income! You'll find hints on easy ways to save on wood and tools, ideas for projects to sell, guidance for handling money and more! Plus, new information on home-business zoning and tax facts keeps you up-to-date. *#70320/$18.99/128 pages/20 b&w illus./paperback*